My Father's Guitar & Other Imaginary Things

My Father's Guitar
& Other Imaginary Things

TRUE STORIES

JOSEPH SKIBELL

ALGONQUIN BOOKS OF CHAPEL HILL 2015

Published by
Algonquin Books of Chapel Hill
Post Office Box 2225
Chapel Hill, North Carolina 27515-2225

a division of
Workman Publishing
225 Varick Street
New York, New York 10014

"International Type of Guy" was published in *Literary Hub*, "If You Were Smiths" was published in a slightly different form as "Everyone's a Critic (Even My Cousin)" in *Poets & Writers*, "My Father's Guitar & Other Imaginary Things" in *The Millions*, a section of "Call Morris" as "Eggheads" in *The Austin Chronicle*, "Don't Mess with Mister In Between" in *Tablet* magazine, "Ten Faces" in *Commentary*, and "Paul McCartney's Phone Number" in the Alan Cheuse Literary Review. "Ten Faces" was also staged as a reading as part of Theater Emory's Brave New Works festival.

Illustration copyright by Jerry Skibell. Used by permission.

"The Hometurning," a screenplay mentioned in "Call Morris," is based on an unpublished short story by James Dennis.

I'm grateful to the Bill and Carol Fox Center for Humanistic Inquiry at Emory University for the time and quiet to work on the final drafts of this book.

"Linda Paloma" written by Jackson Browne. Published by Swallow Turn Music (ASCAP).

Library of Congress Cataloging-in-Publication Data
Skibell, Joseph.
My father's guitar & other imaginary things : true stories /
Joseph Skibell.—First edition.
    pages cm
ISBN 978-1-56512-930-6 (alk. paper)
1. Skibell, Joseph. 2. Novelists, American—20th century—Biography.
3. Authors, American—20th century—Family relationships. 4. Conduct
of life. I. Title.
PS3569.K44Z46 2015
813'.54—dc23
[B]   2015015881

10 9 8 7 6 5 4 3 2 1
First Edition

Though these stories are true—everything that happens in them happened in actual life—I've changed the names of a few of the people who appear in them. I've done this sometimes at their request and sometimes in gentlemanly deference to old lovers and friends. Also, as a work of memory, this book is subject to the distortions, incorrections, and elisions of all retrospection.

in memory of my father,
IRVIN ALFRED SKIBELL,

and for
SPIDER JOHNSON
&
MEREDITH MITCHELL,
with gratitude
for the guitar
and the other imaginary things

At the moment the music began
and you heard the guitar player starting to sing
you were filled with the beauty that ran
through what you were imagining.

—JACKSON BROWNE, "Linda Paloma"

CONTENTS

My Father's Guitar & Other Imaginary Things

MY FATHER'S GUITAR & OTHER IMAGINARY THINGS

It all started about five years ago when I received a call from a colleague. We'd done a bit of work together, planning a new major for the college where we teach, and we'd been compensated for this work with a small bonus to our travel-and-research funds. My colleague was calling to alert me to the fact—something he'd only then discovered—that if these funds weren't spent by the end of that day, they'd be forfeited and returned to the college.

I gathered up all the work-related receipts I could find,

but when I totaled them up, I still had $177 dollars left, and so I did the only thing I could think to do, the only rational thing a person in my situation might do: I went down to my local Guitar Center, flagged down a salesman, told him I had $177 to spend before midnight, and asked him if he'd be willing to part with a Martin Backpacker for that precise amount.

A Martin Backpacker, if you've never seen one, is a small broom-shaped guitar that's light enough to be carried into the woods on a backpacking trip, if you were so inclined. It's also, according to the Martin catalog, the first guitar ever sent into outer space.

The sales guy told me he'd be delighted to sell me the guitar for that price and he went into the back to get one.

This made me extraordinarily happy for two reasons. First, though I started playing at nine years old, I hadn't gotten a new guitar since I was fourteen. I'd been playing less and less over the years, and I was unprepared for the sense of a renewed love affair a new instrument brings with it. Secondly, I retained in my memory a sharply etched image of my father, leaning his large body against the counter of Harrod Music Co. in Lubbock, Texas, bargaining with Clyde, the manager there, over the blue electric Fender Mustang he was buying to replace the clunky Fender acoustic he'd originally brought home for me after I'd mentioned to him that I wanted to learn how to play the guitar.

Big and cumbersome, that acoustic Fender was too

difficult for me to play. The neck was thick and beefy, and the strings were so high you could have hung laundry from them.

As a kid, I was mortified by my father's bargaining. Everywhere else, when you bought something, you paid what they asked for it, but Dad was a businessman, he was a merchant, he understood about markup. Still, I was afraid he might offend Clyde, that this back-and-forthing of theirs might end in a stalemate or, worse, an argument—Dad had an eruptive, unpredictable temper—and I'd lose not only the guitar but Clyde's affection, which would mean having to go elsewhere for my lessons.

My teacher at Harrod's was a lanky hippie iconoclast named Spider Johnson. He was a liberating presence in my young life, and I didn't want to lose contact with him.

I was worried, also, that all this *handln* might seem too Jewish for Clyde or for Mr. Harrod, the patrician owner of the shop. The founding conductor of the Lubbock Symphony Orchestra, Mr. Harrod saw to the violins, while Clyde handled the guitars.

But Clyde, it turned out, was happy for the sale, as was the guy at Guitar Center thirty years later, as was I in both cases. I'm sure it had more to do with my father than with the money, but the forty or so bucks the Guitar Center guy was willing to knock off the Backpacker left me feeling inordinately potent as a man.

I brought the little Martin home, and for my birthday,

my wife, Barbara, gave me a couple of songbooks containing hits from the 1920s and '30s, and I loved nothing better than to sit at our kitchen table late into the night, playing my little broom-shaped guitar and singing songs like "Ain't Misbehavin'," "Bye Bye, Blackbird," and "California, Here I Come!"

My father was hospitalized a year or so after I bought the Backpacker. He was living in Oklahoma City at the time with his second wife—my mother had died years before—and my brother and sisters and I each received a call telling us we'd better get up there to see him. No one expected him to leave the hospital: his kidneys were shot and he had a host of other medical concerns.

"His organs are just plumb wore out," his nephrologist told me.

As soon as we all arrived, Dad went into a coma. At one point, there was even a Code Blue. The machines in his ICU room started whirring. The staff rushed in and pulled the curtains. The hospital chaplain showed up, a fretful-looking woman in a boxy skirt set.

"May I *sit* with you?" she asked each of us in turn, inflecting the verb somehow with overtones of Christian sodality.

"No thanks," we each said.

I have to say, she seemed relieved. Clutching her files to her chest, she sat down, and she disappeared when no one was looking.

As for my sisters and brother and me, we all braced ourselves and waited for our father to die.

BUT DAD DIDN'T DIE.
Contrary to all expectations, he came out of his coma.
Eventually well enough to leave the ICU, he was furloughed
to an ordinary hospital room, and though he spent nearly
sixty days as an inpatient, he was ultimately released.

During those sixty days, whenever I went to visit him, I
brought the little Backpacker along. We didn't have a lot of
common interests, my father and I, our conversation was
often halting and difficult, but music was something we
both loved, and I'd sit by his bedside and play for him. It
helped to pass the hours for both of us, and the odd-shaped
guitar proved a useful conversation piece with the nurses.

I DON'T KNOW what was going on in my father's marriage, but when he left the hospital, he no longer seemed welcome at home. He ended up in Dallas, living in Mrs. Rudd's
condominium. Mrs. Rudd was my uncle Richard's mother-
in-law. Too frail at ninety-something to travel from her home
in Wichita, she no longer used the place, and Dad moved in
in a quiet violation of the condo board's rules, which forbade
any and all subletting.

I continued bringing the little Martin along whenever I
visited—it was so light and easy to pack—and on one occasion, we all sat together as a family in Mrs. Rudd's living

room, my brother-in-law Alan and I taking turns on the guitar. Dad joined in, singing old cowboy and Sammy songs. He seemed to enjoy himself, and one day he told me he thought maybe he'd buy himself a guitar, take a few lessons. Why not? He was retired and living alone with a pair of alternating caregivers. He had the time, and he asked me for advice on what to buy.

I was quite proud of him, proud that, at the age of seventy-six, he was up for something new.

"And if, for some reason, I can't learn it," he said, "I'll give it to you and you can keep it."

THE NEXT TIME I was in Dallas, we all sat around Mrs. Rudd's living room again, singing and playing, and when I took a turn on Dad's new guitar, I remember thinking, *Man, this is a beautiful instrument!* Curvier than most guitars, it was shaped like a figure eight, with the upper bouts (the shoulders) as wide and round as the lower bouts (the hips), and the top, back, and sides all a handsome dark nutty brown.

"That's a dreadnought guitar," my friend Elbein told me when I described it to him after I'd returned home. "Big and boxy?" he said.

I nodded. He seemed to know what he was talking about.

"Yeah, those're called dreadnoughts. After the battleships, because they're so big and boxy, you have to play them standing up."

"Yeah, well, whatever. It's just a beautiful instrument," I said, "and whether my father gives it to me or it comes down to me years from now, I might just hang it on a wall as a symbol of my father's will to keep learning and moving forward, and also because it's just so damned beautiful. I don't think I've ever seen a guitar quite like that before."

As it turns out, Dad's arthritis was too bad for him to pursue the guitar in earnest, and one day, when my daughter, Samantha, and I were in Dallas, he said to me, "Joseph, take that guitar. I'm never going to learn it."

"Really, Dad?"

"Take it, take it!"

"Are you sure?"

"Sure, I'm sure," he said.

"Because it's just such a beautiful guitar."

I was torn. On the one hand, I hated to see him giving up on it. On the other, I was thrilled to have the guitar. But either way, he was adamant, and when we said our good-byes, Samantha carried the guitar out of Mrs. Rudd's condo, while I went to get the car. By the time I drove back to the porte-cochere, she had taken it out of its case and was standing on one foot, balancing it on her raised leg, strumming a few chords.

Hey, that's not my father's guitar! I thought as I pulled up. It wasn't the guitar I remembered at all, the one shaped like an infinity sign with the nutty brown color.

There was nothing special about this guitar, in fact.

It was nothing but a cheap blonde Alvarez!

"HEY, DAD, THAT'S not the original guitar you bought, is it?"

I was sitting next to him that evening at dinner, and I couldn't help asking him the question, although he didn't seem to understand it, which wasn't surprising. The room was noisy, I was sitting on his bad side, and what I was asking him was utterly nonsensical.

"I mean, you didn't buy *two* guitars, did you?"

"No, no."

"Well, but then, I mean, what happened to the first guitar?"

"No, that *is* the first guitar."

Maybe my brother-in-law stole it was my next thought. *Maybe he swapped it out for the Alvarez when he thought no one was looking.*

There were only two problems with this. First, Alan would never have done such a thing—he was too honest—and second, if he had, he'd never have gotten away with it. Eventually, I'd see the guitar in his house.

This was all very problematic for me, mostly because my sisters have always insisted, especially when it comes to family history, that my grasp of reality is—how to put this succinctly?—less than firm, that for me memory and imagination are like two converging rivers, that I tend to misremember things or, more probably, make them up. Now, even I will admit that the two of them seemed to have grown up in an entirely different household from mine. They were born eighteen months apart and because they're close not only in age but in temperament, their versions of our family history tend to match up. At times, we hardly seem to have come from the same family.

For the first time, though, I began to wonder if my sisters hadn't been right after all. I mean, if I could dream a guitar up out of thin air, what else, over the years, had I imagined?

THE MYSTERY OF where this imaginary guitar came from persisted literally for years until, sometime after my father's death, I was taking a walk and the realization struck me with absolute clarity: the first guitar Dad bought me, that clunky, nearly unplayable Fender—the one with the strings so high you could have hung laundry from them—had been figure eight in shape with a handsome nutty-brown color. I'd forgotten all about that guitar, but now I realized that, in a move that was laughably Freudian, filled with wish fulfillment and dreamlike distortions, I'd mentally substituted the *first* guitar my father had given me with the *last* guitar he'd ever give me, hoping in this way, I suppose, to reverse time and keep him alive.

It didn't work, of course.

Though Dad survived his sixty days in the hospital, he died a few years after that. In the wake of his death, I took

Sami on a road trip. We visited various guitar makers, and with a part of my inheritance, I bought a beautiful hand-made archtop, which I named Fig, partly because the figures in its maple back look like the meat of a fig and also because Fig stands for *F*ather's *I*maginary *G*uitar.

And these days, it's with Fig that I sit up late into the night at my kitchen table, often thinking about my father and singing those great old songs from the 1920s and the 1930s, songs like "I Can't Give You Anything but Love" and "Button Up Your Overcoat (You Belong to Me)."

INTERNATIONAL TYPE OF GUY

I don't remember when it occurred to me to ask the telemarketers for money. Like everyone else in those days, we were inundated by their calls. Unsolicited offers for products and services, requests for donations, come-ons for weekend getaways made our phone ring at all hours of the day. These calls registered as "Out of Area" on my Southwestern Bell Freedom Phone caller ID box, and there seemed to be no way of dealing with them other than by not picking up.

Around this same time, I'd purchased a couple of books on the North American Esperanto Association's website, and they arrived accompanied by an enticing brochure someone at the Esperanto headquarters thought to slip into my package announcing the Eighty-Eighth annual Universala Kongreso de Esperanto. It was being held that year in Sweden.

To the derision of almost everyone I knew—my wife and daughter, our friends, even distant relatives and casual acquaintances—I was teaching myself Esperanto, the universal language invented at the end of the nineteenth century by Dr. L. L. Zamenhof, a Warsaw oculist.

In Esperanto, the word *Esperanto* literally means "one who hopes," and it was Dr. Zamenhof's fervent hope that a universal language might usher in an age of international brotherhood and world peace.

Why my friends and family found universal brotherhood and world peace so damnably funny, I have no idea, and when they scoffed at me, as they invariably did, I said to them, "Ha! You see! It works! You're laughing already!"

Persevering like a postman through the snow and the sleet and the gloom of their derision, I diligently worked my way through Cresswell and Hartley's *Teach Yourself Esperanto*, while availing myself of the ten free lessons offered on the association's website.

Depending on who you ask, it's estimated that there are anywhere from a million to eight million speakers of Esperanto in the world, and becoming fluent in Dr. Zamenhof's invented language entitles an Esperantisto to an official

Esperanto passport with which he or she may travel the world, staying free in the homes of *aliaj samideanoj* (literally: same idea sharers). But when I asked the editor of the *New York Times* Sophisticated Traveler to send me to Sweden to cover the conference, though I'd written an article for the magazine on eccentric tourist traps in the American Southwest and another on a one-block-long street in Vienna where both Freud and Herzl had lived, she told me the story was too parochial for their readers.

How can a universal language promoting international brotherhood and world peace be parochial? I wondered. And I saw her refusal to send me to Sweden as further evidence of humanity's decline, the very sort of thing that had disillusioned Dr. Zamenhof and perhaps even led to his early death.

With no sponsor for the trip and unable—or, in truth, unwilling—to pay for it myself, I realized in a flash of inspiration that I could solicit the dozens of telemarketers who called our house every day for the funds I needed. And if I couldn't raise the money for the conference from them—the chances of which seemed slim, even to me—I could at least undermine their incessant monetary demands on me. After all, having refused *me* for *my* cause, how could they expect me to donate to *theirs*? Also, I reasoned, they were calling *me*. As a fund-raiser now myself, I'd simply presume that anyone who voluntarily called my number was doing so out of a desire to donate to my fund. I'd had a phone installed in my house for my convenience, after all, and not theirs.

This changed the entire dynamic of the situation.

I no longer dreaded the telemarketers' calls. Instead, I found myself waiting for them with a keen sense of anticipation. Indeed, I was practically giddy the first time the phone rang and I ran into the kitchen and peered into the little caller ID box and saw the words *Out of Area* flashing on its tiny plasma screen.

I answered the phone and, leaning against the counter, pressed it to my ear. I waited through the telltale silence at the other end of the line, standing by for the telemarketer's computer to connect us so that the telemarketer could utter the incongruous *Hello?* that made it seem as though I had called him and not he me.

"Hello?" a woman's voice finally said.

"Ah! I'm so glad you called," I exclaimed, and I could almost hear her shoulders dropping. *I'm so glad you called*, I imagine, isn't something a telemarketer hears every day. She seemed momentarily at a loss for words. Taking advantage of her silence, I launched into my spiel.

"I'm soliciting funds to send a delegate to the Eighty-Eighth Annual Esperanto Congress in Sweden," I told her, "and I was hoping I could count on your support this year. May I put you down for an eighteen-dollar contribution?"

To be honest, I thought she'd simply hang up on me and

I was surprised by her reaction. She started laughing, and she had a gorgeously vibrant and throaty voice.

"No, you're right, you're right," I said. "Eighteen dollars *is* a laughably small amount for such an important cause. Shall we say thirty-six, then?"

"I can't send you dollars," she said.

"But why not?"

"Because I'm in Canada!" She laughed her glorious laugh.

"Oh, that's okay," I said. "Our critics claim that Esperanto has always been supported by loonies."

"No, I'm sorry, but I don't think I can do it."

She sounded sincerely regretful. She seemed a little starved for conversation, to tell you the truth. She'd probably have talked to me all day, and though she sounded pleasant enough, I had work to do. I was pleased to note, though, that, having refused *me* money, she no longer seemed to feel that she could ask me for any, and she hung up without identifying the company she worked for.

The second telemarketer hung up on me immediately, but the third one, a young man with a foreign accent, sounded intrigued.

"Esperanto?" he said. "What's that?

"Oh, well, thank you for asking," I said to him, propping my feet onto my desk. "Esperanto is an international language designed so that people the world over can easily learn to communicate with one another. Not only would this aid

science and medicine and commerce, of course, but once
people of different cultures are able to communicate fully
with one another, our hearts will open, and we'll be able to
look beyond the barriers that divide us. You know what I'm
talking about: barriers of ethnicity, nationality, creed."

"Well," he said, "I *am* kind of an international type of guy."

He actually said this.

"Ah, well, Esperanto is right up your alley, then, and you
could be proud to help sponsor a delegate."

"Where do I send the check?"

"Where do you send the check?" I said.

"Yeah, where do I send the check?"

"I assume you have my address?"

"Are you still at . . . ?"

Secure in a more familiar script, he rattled off my address.

"I am," I said, "but I can't take your money."

"No?" He sounded hurt. "Why not? I'm an international
type of guy."

"I know, but . . . look, it's . . . it's just . . . I'm sorry, but . . ."

This was too absurd. Once again, I had to beg off, and not
because the telemarketer on the other end of the line was
demanding my money. On the contrary, he wanted to send
me money, and he wanted to talk. And he wanted to talk
about Esperanto! A subject no one in my immediate household or neighborhood or circle of friends or extended family
had the slightest interest in. *What's wrong with me?* Here
was a potential *samideano*, a self-described "international

type of guy," and I was treating him as though he were nothing more than a pesky telemarketer!

What kind of Esperantisto was I?

I had to take stock. I had to take a hard look at myself. Why was it so hard for me to treat these telemarketers as though they were real people whose lives mattered and whose interests might coincide with my own? Most of them were probably fellow writers and actors and musicians trying to cobble together a living while pursuing their under-remunerative arts. I'd had jobs like that before, though—it's true—I was never competent enough to keep them for more than a day or two.

Worse: Dr. Zamenhof would have been ashamed of me, I knew.

Still, I couldn't help noting that, like the Canadian woman before him, this international type of guy neglected to identify his company and he forgot to try to sell me anything.

The next time I asked for a donation, the man on the other end of the line started stammering. "Um, um, um, um, Joseph," he said in a dignified-sounding voice, "I am *so very thrilled* that you have asked me to contribute to this wonderful, this noble cause."

"So I can count on your support, then?"

"No, I don't think so."

"Thank you for calling, anyway," I said.

"No, thank *you*, sir. Thank *you*. And you have yourself a wonderful, no, a marvelous evening."

He, too, neglected to identify his company, and I was able to get off the phone without feeling either bilked or guilty for having turned down a good cause. Even more, I was pleased to see that this simple act of stepping out from behind the masks we wear—he playing the ambushing telemarketer; I, the besieged householder—had an enlivening effect on us both.

In the end, though, I couldn't keep it up. There were too many telemarketers, and these conversations were proving too time-consuming. I barely had enough energy for the people in my life who mattered to me. I couldn't be available for every Tom, Dick, and Harry with a phone book.

Dr. Zamenhof wasn't like this, of course. A gentle utopian dreamer, he gave of himself to everyone who crossed his path, seeing to his patients during the day, treating the poorer ones for no fee or in exchange for milk or butter or eggs, while working late into the night, first to create and then to promote, as a gift for all humankind, a universal language so that the man-made borders that divide us might be crossed, and the human heart, which we too often hold closed, like a fist, against our fellows, might open, and the world's wealth—our material, spiritual, and cultural heritage—might be shared with all its inhabitants, ushering in an epoch of universal brotherhood and peace.

What's so funny about that? I still want to know.

Dr. Zamenhof was so beloved, in fact, that when he died in 1917 at the age of fifty-eight, droves of mourners accompanied his coffin to the Warsaw Jewish Cemetery, and many of the poorer folk among them had no idea that their simple, saintly doctor had invented an artificial language and led an international movement that had spread that language all over the world.

These days, it seems, we only talk to one another when we need something. It's as though we've all become telemarketers, pestering each other for the recognition and the love we need. American life is so fundamentally economic that it's hard to justify doing something that doesn't have an economic advantage to it: sitting with friends, chatting with a stranger on the phone, learning a silly made-up language for the sake of world peace.

Now whenever I get a call from Out of Area, I let the phone ring, and as the ringing fills my house, I can't help thinking that Dr. Zamenhof was right. We do need a new way of speaking to each other. But a universal language isn't enough. It's our hearts that must answer the call.

IF YOU WERE SMITHS

I didn't ask him to do it, but on his own, my cousin posted one of those customer reviews of my second novel on Amazon.com. I've always been wary of those pithy critiques that anyone can post on book-selling websites, suspecting that writers ask their friends and relatives to send in ecstatic responses to their books under various pseudonyms, and I was reluctant to involve myself in what, at heart, seemed a deception, and not because I believe in the Invisible Hand of the Free Market either. I don't assume that every deserving book will find its audience, that every worthy novel will create its own hullabaloo. It's more that I know that these reviews, written by an author's relatives and friends, never convince anyone.

I learned this lesson early.

When I was kid, among the commercial properties my family owned was a restaurant called Hobo Joe's. The name always mystified me. Who'd want to eat a meal cooked by a hobo? The sign featured a black-and-white drawing of a miserable fellow dressed in rags, smoking a cigar that he held to his mouth on the end of a toothpick. The place had been originally a Denny's, and it had had several incarnations after that, all of them unspectacularly profitless. My family wanted to get rid of it, but buyers were few and far between.

Late one afternoon, though, I came home and my sister Cindy told me, "Hurry up and get dressed. We're going to Hobo Joe's."

"But why?" I said. "It's a horrible restaurant."

"I know, but there's a buyer," she said. "Now come on!"

It's no good showing an empty restaurant to a potential buyer, so Skibells were summoned from across the city, commanded by patriarchal fiat to appear at Hobo Joe's at the dinner hour. We were the only people there, but we're a large family and we filled the booths and the tables. When we saw my father and my uncle Albert through the plate-glass windows getting out of a car in the parking lot with a stranger in tow, we ceased shouting across the restaurant to one another and spoke to our tablemates in hushed tones, appropriate for dinner conversation, instead.

What the buyer saw, as my uncle and father showed him the salad bar and the kitchen, was a crowded restaurant full of people who more or less resembled one another: olive-skinned Jews with curly dark hair and dark eyes, all of them pretending not to see the three men conducting business in their midst.

No one was fooled, and all we got for our trouble was an inedible meal.

AND SO IT was with a certain amount of trepidation, if not outright dread, that I read the email from my cousin Jeremy complimenting me on my new book and informing me that not only had he enjoyed the novel but he had posted his own review of it on Amazon.com.

"Nothing wrong with a little shilling," he said.

A little shilling? I thought. *Get dressed, we're going to Hobo Joe's!*

I immediately logged onto the website and looked up my book, and there, as promised, was Jeremy's review. I have to say, my cousin was lavish with his praise. Titling his critique "A Positively Great Read," he gave the book five stars. He made the odd claim that the book came highly recommended (*By whom?* I wondered. *By his father? By my father?*), stating in conclusion that "the internal monologues are so readable and funny, they make the book worth it on their own."

Unfortunately, due to a technical glitch on the website, the critique was signed not only with his first but also with his last name, which, of course, is my last name, and so his review appeared to be exactly what it was: a little shilling.

NOT LONG AFTER that, at the rehearsal dinner for a family wedding in Dallas, Jeremy's mother approached me.

"You know Jeremy wrote a nice review for you on Amazon .com, don't you?"

"Yes, I know," I said, "but unfortunately, it's signed with his own name."

Aunt Janice's brow creased.

"Well, that's no good. I'll have to tell him. He'll have to change it."

The next evening, at the reception following the wedding, Aunt Janice took me by the arm. "Don't worry," she said. "I spoke with Jeremy this afternoon, and he said he'd fix the name thing, and he mentioned that he also left you a review on the Barnes & Noble website."

"Did he?" My heart sank. "How very nice of him."

THE NEXT MORNING, at my sister Cindy's house, I checked BN.com on the computer in her kitchen. Once again, Jeremy gave the book five stars, and this time, he signed the review with only his first name. Here, though, for some reason, he saw fit to quibble with the novel, specifically with the internal monologues he had praised in his earlier review, writing, "Some of the tangents don't work as well as others."

Oh, so this is how he gets even with me for embarrassing him in front of his mother! I thought. *I made him look foolish for signing his own name, and now he takes his revenge?*

I searched through my Yahoo! account to see if I had his email address. I didn't. I looked to see if there were any e-pistles from relatives who might have sent out a bulk mailing that included him as well as me. There was one from my uncle Bernard, and there it was, his email address, Jeremy @zillium.com. Before I knew what I was doing, I had sent him an angry note. Beneath the heading *PLEASE STOP DOING ME FAVORS!!!*, I wrote:

> Dear Jeremy,
> It's bad enough you signed your own name to the Amazon .com reader's review—but to fucking quibble with the fucking book on the fucking Barnes & Noble page—are you fucking crazy!!! Get some sense into your head and stop fucking with my livelihood!!!
> Joseph

A few hours later, I got on a plane and flew home to Atlanta. I anxiously checked my email upon my return. As expected, there was a reply from Jeremy@zillium.com. I opened it nervously, regretting that I'd lost my temper. Still, I was unprepared for what I read next.

"You must have the wrong Jeremy," the message said, "because I don't know you and I didn't write any reviews of your books."

It was signed *Jeremy Rivenburgh*.

I immediately sent Jeremy Rivenburgh a reply under the subject heading *AI-YI-YI!*

> **Dear Mr. Rivenburgh,**
>
> So sorry! I thought you were a cousin of mine. Please forgive me!

"Maybe Rivenburgh's Jeremy's pseudonym," Barbara said. "Maybe he's finally using one."

I next sent an email to Jeremy's father, my uncle Benjamin, asking for Jeremy's email address, and he wrote me back almost immediately. The correct address was JeremyS @zillium.com. The address I'd copied from Uncle Bernard's bulk mailing had dropped the *S*. I wanted to resend the note, but Barbara convinced me not to.

"This is the kind of thing," she said, "that can split up families forever."

For a moment, I considered taking the risk, but then, reluctantly, I agreed.

And the next time I checked my email, I was surprised to see that Jeremy Rivenburgh had responded to my apologetic note:

Hey, no problem. Your mail certainly stood out from a mail-box full of spam, I must say. Give my regards to your idiot cousin. You're right, though, he really shouldn't sign those reviews with his last name. If you were Smiths, it'd be different! :)

Jeremy

CALL MORRIS

During the seven years I spent struggling as a screenwriter in Los Angeles, my father constantly implored me to call Morris. "Call Morris," he said, again and again, as though this single call might put an end to all my professional woes.

"Call Morris. Why don't you call Morris?" he'd say.

But calling Morris was something I resisted doing. I'm not sure why. I was too shy, for one thing, too timid to reach out to a relative I barely knew. Also, my father and I had a complicated relationship, and I'm sure that had something to do with it. Dad and I lived in different worlds; the rules of his world didn't seem to apply in mine, and whenever I followed his advice, the results were semidisastrous.

My first professional writing assignment, for instance, was for *Rolling Stone* magazine. Right out of college, I was commissioned to write a piece on how Lubbock remembered Buddy Holly, its most famous—and, at the time, famously neglected—son.

Dad insisted I wear a coat and a tie to conduct the interviews in.

"You're representing the family," he said.

"Actually, Dad, I'm representing *Rolling Stone* magazine."

"Change," he said. "You can't go out of the house looking like that."

To please him, I did the interviews, stiff and uncomfortable, in slacks and a tie, and the story never ran.

Another time, when a hard-bitten New York agent turned down my plays, Dad suggested I send her flowers. I can still remember her poisonous little thank-you note: *Little yellow roses: how dainty, how ladylike.*

I was leery about following his advice, but even more, his invoking Morris confused me. You have to understand: from the moment I announced as a teenager that I wanted to be a writer, my father initiated a vehement counter campaign against those ambitions. You'd have thought I'd chosen lechery and chicanery as a career path, so dire were the predictions he painted of my prospects: an uncertain life of poverty and the unmasculine humiliations associated with the inability to provide for your wife and children. All through my adolescence, he attempted to argue, wheedle, reason, cajole, persuade, hector, lecture, and frighten me out of what I, with a teenage purity of heart, considered a noble calling, and whenever he sensed he was losing the argument, he pulled Morris out as his trump card.

"Look at your uncle Ike," he'd say. "Look at Tiger! Look at Morris Berger, for God's sakes! Is that really the kind of life you want for yourself?"

IKE, TIGER, MORRIS: these were the ne'er-do-wells, the *luftmenschen*, of our family. Ike was my mother's kid brother. He hadn't made much of himself, I suppose it's true. He'd worked behind an airline counter at O'Hare for a while after college but quit to take care of his mother, and he lived with her, escorting her here, escorting her there, until she died.

Tiger was Jack Tiger, my father's first cousin, a filmmaker manqué and a bit of a flim-flam man.

Morris was Morris Berger, a distant cousin on my mother's side. In the late 1950s, Morris went out to Hollywood. He changed his name to Jeff Morris and became an actor, playing small parts on television in westerns like *Bonanza* and *Death Valley Days* and later in the movies.

When I was a kid, Dad occasionally called me into the

den and pointed at our television set. "There's your cousin," he'd say, gesturing towards a lanky, long-faced, blond-haired man, more often than not in a cowboy hat.

In my father's view, these men—Ike, Tiger, Morris— were not serious men. They had no money—that was one thing—but even more, they did no work. Or no real work. They lived their lives like children. They lived *children's* lives, lives without heft, without weight, without burden or responsibility.

"Jerry Janger had the sense to realize that acting was a game," my father invariably told me during these conversations, "fun to play at maybe, but based entirely on chance, on luck, on fate."

Jerry Janger was another one of our cousins. He'd won a Mr. Texas Formal contest at the University of Texas in the early 1950s and, as part of his prize, was given a screen test. Taken on by one of the studios, he appeared in an episode of *Father Knows Best* and in a movie called *Rumble on the Docks*, but then he was drafted. When he returned from the service, the world had moved on. The people who knew him at the studio were no longer there, and he became a lawyer instead.

"Now Jerry did the sensible thing," my father often told me, "and he has no regrets. But Morris . . . Morris never grew up and now just look at him: unmarried, no children, no solid career to his name. What kind of life is that? Is that the kind of life you want?"

Of course, it wasn't the kind of life I wanted, but neither

was my father's. In all honesty, my father's life, the life of a small-town businessman, appeared equally unenviable. Dad had been on his way to the University of Chicago for a PhD in industrial psychology, a young field back then, when, for reasons that were never fully explained to me, he changed his mind and went to work in the family business instead.

Our family owned a small fleet of ladies' ready-to-wear stores across Texas called Skibell's.

When I was growing up, Dad hardly seemed the happiest of men—I rarely saw him in a good mood, to tell you the truth—though I knew enough not to use that as an argument in my defense.

"Oh, no, no, but you're happy enough that I can afford to buy you a bicycle and a guitar and pay for your lessons and send you off to Europe on a People to People tour . . ." I knew he'd say.

And so now, all these years later, it was strange to hear him urging me to call Morris, a little strange, if not impossible, for me to declassify Morris as a poor role model, as a ne'er-do-well, as a *luftmensch*, and reclassify him as a man on the inside, a relative with clout, an important contact it might behoove me to call.

"Bob says he's in with important people," Dad told me, "that he's got important friends."

Bob was Morris' brother, Dr. Robert Berger. The two served as a kind of Jekyll-and-Hyde pair in my adolescent understanding of the world. Both had left Lubbock for glamorous

Southern California and, though Morris, presumably, was miserable, living hand to mouth, Bob was a well-respected gastroenterologist with a beautiful wife, a swimming pool, and a thriving practice in La Jolla.

As far as Morris' important friends went, these included principally—my father told me—Jack Nicholson. Morris, in fact, appears in seven or eight of Nicholson's films, though usually not for more than a line or two, a couple of small scenes, just enough, I suspected, to keep him a member in good standing in the Screen Actors Guild so that he could continue receiving health insurance.

I was on a plane not long ago, half watching *Anger Management*, when Morris' face suddenly filled the screen. Nicholson plays Dr. Buddy Rydell, an unconventional anger management counselor who, assigned to Adam Sandler's case, moves into Sandler's apartment to undertake an extreme cure. Dr. Rydell's assistant, a tall man in hipsterish black, carries in Rydell's suitcases. Leaning a massage table against a wall, Morris delivers his single line in extreme close-up: "Anything else, Dr. B.?"

I MET MORRIS only once. I was nine years old when he came to Lubbock to visit his parents, Hazel and Abe. He had a small role in a movie called *Kelly's Heroes*, a World War II spoof starring Clint Eastwood, Donald Sutherland, Telly Savalas, and Carroll O'Connor. As far as Lubbock was concerned, though, Morris was a bona fide movie star. There was even an article about the local boy making good in the *Avalanche-Journal* with a picture of Morris and Abe standing outside the Arnett Benson Theatre.

My mother drove my brother Ethan and me over to the Bergers' so we could get Morris' autograph. I was a thin little boy with bangs, wearing a favorite blue cardigan, as I recall. Morris signed two eight-by-ten-inch black-and-white glossies as "Jeff Morris" and handed one to each of us. In the picture, he's in character, in an army uniform, sitting in what looked like an army barracks. He seemed embarrassed by the whole thing, to tell you the truth, annoyed by it, bothered. I asked him if he could recite any of his lines from the movie, but he said he couldn't remember them.

"You can't *remember* them?" I said.

I thought remembering lines was what an actor did, but Morris told me it takes a long time, sometimes years and years, to make a movie and even longer sometimes for it to come out. He'd made *Kelly's Heroes* a year and a half ago, and there was no way he could remember his lines now, and this seemed plausible enough to me until I went to the Arnett Benson and saw the movie and saw that Morris only had a few lines.

In one scene, a battle scene in France—which *I* can still remember—an outhouse falls on Don Rickles and Harry Dean Stanton, both playing members of Morris' battalion.

"Oooh-weee, you boys fall into a cow patch or sum'pin?" Morris says to them.

"Kinda makes you homesick, doesn't it?" Rickles snaps in frustration, before stomping off.

Morris and Stanton—their characters are simple country boys—look at each other sheepishly.

"Kinda does, dudn't it?" Stanton says.

"Yeah," Morris admits.

MY UNCLE IKE and Morris had been friends as kids. Ike used to come to Lubbock from Chicago to visit Morris, and it always struck me as strange—the way normal things strike children as strange—that Ike had been in Lubbock long before my mother, who would live her entire adult life there, ever set foot in the city.

Nothing strange about that, I realize this now. Cousins visit cousins, and cousins' sisters sometimes marry cousins' friends, especially in Lubbock, where marriageable Jewish women did not then and do not now grow on trees. When I was a kid, though, the thought that my Chicagoan uncle had walked and run and rode minibikes along the dusty streets of my hometown long before my parents married, long before Dad brought Mom there to live, long before my sisters and brother and I were all born, seemed like a miraculous instance of a life foretold.

The two cousins remained close. In the summer of 1958,

Ike even drove with Morris halfway to LA when Morris lit out for Hollywood. Barely eighteen, they spent a week gambling in Vegas before Ike returned to Chicago and Morris pushed on through the mountains into LA alone.

They kept up through the years, and once when I was in Chicago, Ike told me that Morris had called him recently. He'd been in town filming *The Blues Brothers* with John Belushi and Dan Aykroyd.

At the time—this was probably 1978 or '79—Ike was living in his sister Adelle's condominium on North Lake Shore Drive, sleeping on the pull-out sofa in her living room. This was only a temporary measure, of course. Their mother had died a few years before. After her funeral Ike disappeared, and no one knew where he was until about six weeks later when he washed up in New Orleans with no money and no idea what had happened to his car.

"Hey, man, I'm here at the Drake with some of my friends," Morris said to Ike the night he called. "Whyn't you come over and join us? We've got some killer blow."

Sitting on Adelle's pull-out sofa—it was pushed in now, of course—Ike told me the story, playing the role of Morris, his hand near his cheek as though it were a phone.

"Really?" I said, leaning forward in my chair.

"Oh, yeah," Ike said.

"And did you go?"

"Of course not."

"You didn't *go?*"

"No, of course not."

"Why didn't you go?"

He raised and lowered a single shoulder.

This made no sense to me. I was nineteen or twenty at the time. Belushi and Aykroyd were *huge*.

"And what did you say to Morris then? I mean, what did you tell him? What happened after that?"

"What happened after that?"

"Yeah, I mean, what happened after that?"

Ike mimed hanging up the phone.

"You *hung up* on him!"

Ike shrugged again.

"But *why?*" I said.

"What'd he think, that he could impress me with all of that stuff?"

I sat back in my chair. The light off Lake Michigan poured through the tall windows into the room. This wasn't how I imagined the story ending. It seemed a strange way to treat a cousin, a strange way to treat a friend. I looked at Ike, sitting on Adelle's pull-out sofa, his arms crossed, one leg over the other. He seemed pleased with himself, pleased with the moment in its retelling, vindicated, as though hanging up on Morris had been the self-evidently correct thing to do.

MY OWN CAREER in Hollywood proved a total fiasco. I'd come to LA thinking I could support my serious literary work with the easy money I'd make as a screenwriter, an idea based on a complete misunderstanding of reality. For some reason, it hadn't occurred to me that I'd be competing for writing jobs with people who *actually* wanted to make movies and that this might give them an edge.

Still, things had started out promisingly enough. Not long out of college, I'd written a screenplay called "The Home-turning" about a philosophy professor who returns home to Texas for Christmas only to discover that his redneck family have, in his absence, become Hare Krishnas and are going about their lives in the Texas oil fields wearing saffron robes and quoting, chapter and verse, from the Bhagavad Gita.

In the early 1980s, Krishnas were in every airport in the country, and saffron robes, I thought, would be dazzlingly cinematic. Against all expectations, after only a few weeks in town, I had a manager and an agent at the William Morris Agency. The manager represented actors like John Malkovich and Willem Dafoe—I was their first literary client—and the agent was a tiny woman who pounded her fist against the top of her enormous desk when we met and proclaimed, "This film *will* be made."

She had read my script the night before, she told me, and she couldn't put it down. "I've never laughed so hard in bed."

Sitting across the enormous desk from her, I bit my tongue, suppressing the thousand and one snappy come-backs that were on the tip of it.

But saffron robes, it turned out, weren't dazzlingly

cinematic, and no one wanted to make a movie about Gita-thumping rednecks in the Texas oil patch. At every meeting I took, producer after producer told me how much they *loved* the script, how *original* it was, how *funny* and *new* and *bold*, before wondering if I couldn't perhaps write something, well, a little less . . . *weird*.

There was a movie out called *Educating Rita* that was a big hit at the time.

"Couldn't you write something a little bit more like, well, I don't know, like *Educating Rita*?" they all said. "Have you seen it yet? Oh, it's wonderful!"

I tried. I really did. I did everything these producers asked of me. I saw *Educating Rita*. I bought a VHS machine, so I could watch movies at home. I even bought a television set—Barbara and I had lived for years in the mountains of New Mexico without one—so that we could use the VHS machine. I wrote two more screenplays, but I was too young as a writer. I had no craft. I had no control over what I was writing. I was like a character in a short story by I. B. Singer and Nathanael West, a Hollywood writer possessed by the wicked imp of a French surrealist, and the more I tried to write *Educating Rita*, the weirder my scripts became.

The next one, "Eggheads," was a 1930s-style screwball comedy about a playwright who, in order to pay off his gambling debts after a Broadway flop, is forced to work for a Hollywood studio with Kafka, Freud, and Einstein as his collaborators. It was a more or less symbolic representation of my mental state at the time, but at 134 pages, it was too long for Hollywood.

"It's as long as the Bible," one producer complained to me.

Still, it was a Sylvester Stallone movie compared to my next script, "Tales." "Tales" took place in nineteenth-century Germany. It involved a ménage-à-trois between the Brothers Grimm and Dortchen, the wife of Wilhelm Grimm. The three Grimms had, in fact, lived their entire adult lives in one house together, and the story, narrated from within Dortchen Grimm's womb by the yet-to-be-born child of this plural marriage, was, I thought, a tender meditation on innocence and experience.

The one producer who showed interest in it couldn't even sell it to German television, and even I began to realize I was never going to make it in Hollywood. I was never going to write *Educating Rita* or anything like it. My agent and managers were losing interest in me. No one was returning my calls.

I had one last meeting at the Disney Studios. I drove through the gate and parked under a replica of the Parthenon supported not by graceful caryatids but by statues of the Seven Dwarfs and made my way to the producer's bungalow.

This was right around the time of the First Gulf War. Someone had procured a small black-and-white television set with a crooked antenna, and it was sitting on a coffee table in the foyer of the producer's office when I came in. The producer, his assistant, and I—all Jews—watched in horror as Saddam Hussein's Scuds fell on Tel Aviv.

"You still want to have this meeting?" the producer asked me with a grimace.

"I don't know. What do you think?" I said. "I mean, I guess so."

And the three of us trooped dutifully into his office and took our seats. His assistant brought her notepad out and crossed her legs, preparing to write. I pitched my ideas. I don't remember what they were.

The producer nodded his head. "They're thin," he told me.

"Thin? Okay, thin. So how do we fatten them up?"

"You can't," he said. "They're thin."

But thin things become fat all the time, I thought.

Illustrating her boss's point, the assistant brought up Capra.

I brightened at the name. "Ah! You mean Fritjof Capra, the author of *The Tao of Physics*?" a book I happened to be reading at the time.

"No, she means *Frank* Capra," the producer said.

"I meant Frank Capra," the assistant said.

"The movie director," the producer clarified.

His assistant gave me a sweetly pitying look.

"Right, right." I nodded. *"Frank* Capra, the movie director. *It's a Wonderful Life, Mr. Smith Goes to Washington . . ."*

I don't even speak the language here, I thought. *Here, where thin things cannot become fat and Capra is Frank and not Fritjof.*

BARBARA AND I were living in a little bungalow off Windward Circle near Venice Beach, and I drove home, along the 10, in a funk. What was I doing here? I'd wasted years of my life. I didn't even want to be a screenwriter. I wanted to be a playwright, and maybe not even a playwright but a novelist. At the very least, I wanted to be a playwright and a novelist who had reluctantly sold his extraordinary talents out to the movies, but as usual, I'd gotten everything backwards. I hadn't sold out. Who was I kidding? I was try-ing to buy in, and not doing a very good job of it.

I stood inside our ramshackle beach house, filled with its odds and ends of cheap furniture, its shelves overflow-ing with books and record albums, my bicycle stashed in-doors so no one would steal it. Barbara was out working. She wouldn't be home for hours. She had a real job. I tended bar one night a week at the LA Tennis Club, and this was all the money I contributed to our household economy.

Nearing thirty, I was a complete and utter failure as a man. My father was right. I was living the life he feared I would live: an unmasculine life of poverty and professional humiliation. I threw myself on the couch. I told myself I should take a walk on the beach to clear my head, but instead I picked up the phone and did the only thing I could think to do.

I called Morris.

My father had given me his number, and I'd copied it into my address book the way a spy keeps a tab of cyanide hidden on his body: for use in a dire emergency. This was that dire emergency, I told myself. The line rang. A gruff voice answered. I can't remember now if I addressed him as "Jeff" or as "Morris," but I remember not knowing which name to use.

I explained who I was.

"And I just thought I'd call and say hello, you know, because I'm out here writing screenplays and . . ."

"Oh, sure, you're Irvin and Shirlene's son, right?"

"Yeah, that's right."

"And you know I was real close friends with your uncle, didn'ya?"

"Yeah, I think I knew that, yeah."

"Yeah, and did you know that I called him once when I was in Chicago?"

"I may have heard about that, I think."

"And you know what he did to me?"

"Well . . . I mean . . ."

"He hung up on me."

"I mean, he may have mentioned that to me, now that I think of it, yeah."

"Sumabitch hangs up on me. Hangs up the goddamn phone! I'm in Chicago, filming with Belushi and Aykroyd, y'understand? I call him up. I invite him out, and the sumabitch hangs up on me. I knew him since we were kids, y'understanding me and the goddamn sumabitch hangs up on . . . He's a faggot, dy'know that? Well, at least that's what my father told me. Him *and* his sister. Both of 'em faggots. Never married. What my folks said. They warned me against him, my dad did anyway. Didn't want me spendin' time with him. But I'm doin' all right, y'understand? I got work. I got friends. I've got *important* friends. *Influential* friends, you know what I'm saying. Take care of me. They take real good care of me. They look out for me, very influential people."

"Yeah, well, Morris, okay," I said. "I just thought I'd call and say hello, you know, because I'm out here trying to write screenplays and . . ."

"You tell your uncle you talked to me, a'right?"

"Okay."

"And you tell him I told you all a'this."

I DIDN'T, OF course. I never mentioned it to Ike. I never mentioned it to anyone, in fact, until now. The next time my father implored me to call Morris, I told him that I had, that it hadn't proved helpful, and he finally let it drop.

I hung up the phone, my head pounding and with Morris' voice ringing in my ear, I went for a walk along the beach. There's something soothing about Venice Beach in the late afternoon: the slanting light, the cool air, the seagulls wheeling in the sky, the surf pushing against the sand, Harry Perry rolling along on his skates with his puffy turban and his electric guitar, while the sun drops undiligently into the sea.

Walking along the shore that day, there was so much I didn't understand. I didn't understand my uncle's troubled life. As it turned out, Ike would spend more than twenty years sleeping on Adelle's pull-out sofa, living as an unwanted stowaway in her condominium while working as a deliveryman for a medical lab. As the years went by, the two of them became like an unmarried married couple, spending every evening together, traveling to Lubbock together, Ike squiring his elder sister the way he'd squired their mother. They were like characters in a long-running sitcom, aging in their unchanging parts, performing their no longer quite so humorous shtick with a rigid sense of determination, Ike referring ironically to Adelle as "my landlady," Adelle referring to Ike with a certain exasperation as "the tenant."

Unbeknownst at least to the children in our family, Ike had struggled with addiction nearly his entire life. Though he was more or less sober for the twenty years following their mother's death, after Adelle died, he fell—once again and spectacularly—off the wagon, blazing through a quarter of a million dollars of crack before the family realized what was going on.

Suddenly, the ghostly nonstory of his 1976 disappearance began to take on form and substance: a man's mother dies, he disappears, no one knows where he is for six weeks, until he washes up in New Orleans with no money and no car. I mean, how hard is it to find the drug addict in this picture?

At the time, though, all I remember being told was: "He took his mother's death *very* hard."

It was Morris' bad luck that he called and attempted to entice Ike out to the Drake with all that Hollywood cocaine when Ike was only a few years away from his long Lost Weekend in New Orleans. The drugs were the least of it, I imagine. Worse would have been comparing himself, a forty-four-year-old man clinging to the life raft of his sister's pull-out sofa, to Morris, an actor in a major Hollywood film, surrounded by his famous friends in a regal hotel suite with a mountain of the world's best cocaine laid out, like an offering to the bitch-goddess Success, on the glass coffee table.

Recently, I watched Morris' films, most of them for the first time, and I realized that, perhaps based on my father's disdain, I'd misjudged him. He wasn't the stiff amateur I always imagined him to be, helped into films by influential friends so that he might keep his SAG card and his insurance. No, he was a wonderful character actor who, it's clear from his oddly musical performances, thought deeply about his work. His films were almost all major films, and over the course of his long career, he acted in scenes with some of his generation's most notable performers: Nicholson and Eastwood but also Meryl Streep, Harvey Keitel, Mary Steen-burgen, Danny DeVito, Tom Waits, and even Elvis Presley.

As I watched his films, one after another, late into the night, on the TV and VCR Barbara and I had bought nearly twenty-five years before in LA, I began to understand Morris' bitterness towards Ike. Morris had done the impossible. He'd made it! He'd broken into the movies, and when he called Ike, I'm sure all he wanted was for Ike to share this vision of his success with him. Who but Ike could glory with him in his arrival at the top of the Big Rock Candy Mountain? Not the workaday grinds in Lubbock, like my father, who shook their heads at the mention of his name, wondering why he couldn't be more like his brother, Bob.

An unfortunate stalemate: the conditions under which Morris was asking for Ike's admiration were precisely the conditions that prevented Ike from giving it to him. My father and I regarded each other across a similar chasm of incomprehension. As a kid, there was so much I didn't understand about my father's life. I didn't understand the unhappiness that seemed to dog him or his dissatisfaction with the world or the disdain he felt for those relatives of ours who weren't quite making it, and he didn't understand that his concern for me, his terrible fears about my future, felt by me as disapproval, only drove me more resolutely on.

Still, we rarely get the kind of love we want, and though it's easy to grow bitter over the imperfect love we're given, there's nothing to do but accept it.

THE HANK WILLIAMS SONGBOOK

I worked for a few weeks at the Big Texan Steak Ranch in Lubbock when I was fifteen years old. This was the place where, if you ate a seventy-two-ounce steak with all the trimmings—baked potato, buttered bread, salad, ice tea, I forget what else—you got your meal free.

"And you know who can actually do it?" the manager told me after I'd been hired. "This goin'ta surprise you, but cheerleaders. Yeah," he said, "high school cheerleaders. Itty-bitty little girls that jump around all day."

I wasn't old enough to drive, so my mother had to drop

me off and pick me up. I'd lug my guitar case into the back room, tune up, put on a cowboy hat. The place was huge. It was supposed to look like a ranch with bales of hay stacked in the corners and wrought-iron wagon wheels and branding irons and pairs of spurs hung up all over the walls.

James, the other guitarist, and I strolled from room to room and table to table as a country duo. I didn't actually know that many country songs, but I could follow James on whatever he played. Occasionally, we got a request from a teenager dining with her parents for a song by Cat Stevens or Bread, and then James followed me, although we weren't really supposed to play anything but country music. Once—somebody had probably requested a Beatles song—I even played George Harrison's "All Things Must Pass," that dour dirge to vanishing love and existential impermanence.

The silence that followed my solo performance—James didn't recognize the Esus4 and the Asus2 chords and let me play it alone—was broken only when the mother at the table, her hair piled high in a honey-colored beehive, said, "Thay's real sad."

I loved playing for the patrons. I loved strolling from table to table, singing at the top of my lungs. I loved all those crazy country tunes about love gone wrong and lonesome train whistles and blue eyes crying in the rain, songs I'd never learned but somehow always knew, songs like "I'm So Lonesome I Could Cry" and "Why Don't You Love Me?"—which together, when you think about it, have exactly the same themes as "All Things Must Pass."

I was thrilled to be out there, but not James. James was more than twice my age, and he'd sit in the back during our breaks, pulling on a cigarette and staring into space, his black Stetson pushed to the back of his head, his funk belied by the jaunty lavender kerchief he wore around his neck. I have no idea what dark inner visions he was seeing, but the terrible unhappiness I felt emanating from him seemed bleak, adult, vaguely sexual, and way beyond the powers of my teenage comprehension.

"Come on, James!" I remember telling him one night. "Our break's been over now for nearly fifteen minutes! Don't you want to get out there and play for the people?"

But James ignored me. He continued staring into space, and not long after that I was fired. I hadn't quite realized that, for all practical purposes, he was my boss.

I ran into him two weeks later when my mom brought me by to pick up my final check.

"Sorry it didn't work out," he said. "I guess ya just didn't know enough country tunes."

"Yeah," I told him. "I'm thinking about buying *The Hank Williams Songbook.*"

I'd seen it in the racks at Harrod Music Co.

This seemed to simultaneously amuse and distress James.

"You do that," he said, looking at me from the depths of

his despairing blue eyes, the ghost of Hank Williams, dead at twenty-nine in the backseat of a Cadillac at the Skyline Drive-In outside Oak Hill, West Virginia, no doubt imposing itself between us. "You do that. You learn them songs and then you come back here and you give it another try."

"I will," I told him, but of course I never did.

I never even bought the book.

SEX LIVES OF
OUR CHILDREN

Translating the French road signs, our GPS leads us straight to the hotel in Montreal. It's a bit on the *très chic* side, but after the place in Toronto—unidentifiable stains in the sink, toenail clippings on the carpet—I'm happy to pay a little extra. The staff seems friendly, ebullient even. A young French guy—blond hair, Gallic face, Buddy Holly glasses; in fact, he looks like a blond French Buddy Holly, if you can imagine such a thing—carries our bags to the room.

Leading us through the halls, he tells us that the hotel

is over 150 years old, and when I tip him, he wishes me *"et Madame Skibell"* a pleasant stay.

"Mademoiselle *Skibell!*" I correct him. *"C'est ma fille!"*

I look at my daughter, Samantha. With twelve years of Hebrew, but no Romance languages, she's deaf to the nuances we're parsing.

"Ah," the bell man says, *"parlez-vous français?"*

"Oui," I tell him, *"un peu, ober très mal."*

He gives me a strange look, and it's only after I've closed the door that I realize *ober* is Yiddish and not French.

When asked how many foreign languages he could speak, Booker T. Washington is reported to have said, "I can remain silent in seven."

I can—and probably should—remain silent in five, and since two of those five are Yiddish and Esperanto—Barbara chides me that I'm a master of dead languages—it's not like there's anyone to talk to anyway.

Dreamers and ghosts, mostly.

Samantha and I settle in. The room, on the second floor overlooking the street, is spacious, with two large beds and fluffy white pillows. Music drifts in through the open window. I step out onto the balcony. There's a violinist on the street corner with a case full of coins at his feet.

Sami throws herself onto one of the beds. Logging onto her computer, she performs an adolescent magic trick, disappearing into it completely. I sit at the table and try to figure out what's been happening with my credit card. It stopped working somewhere between Toronto and Montreal. I call my bank to straighten things out, but since, thanks to the worldwide economic downturn, my bank is in the process of becoming another bank, I end up talking to a series of bankers, each of whom puts me in touch with another banker.

It turns out you have to inform your bank when you leave the country, and if you don't, the last thing you want to do is pay for gas with a credit card at a pump. Big Brother *is* watching you, but he has a short attention span and no understanding of narrative. Despite a charge for a rental car in Buffalo and a hotel in Toronto, our getting gas in the middle of Canada was economically suspicious.

FOLLOWING OUR CONCIERGE'S recommendation, we take the metro to a nearby vegetarian restaurant. We ascend to the street level at sunset and the city is glowing with a tawny, crepuscular light. Sami graduated from high school only this week, but she's dressed up, and I wonder if here, too, people assume we're a couple. *Don't we look like father and daughter? Is there no family resemblance at all?* I wonder. *At forty-nine, do I really look like a man who might have an eighteen-year-old wife? (And if so, is that a good thing or a bad thing?)*

We're seated, I order a beer, and Samantha mischievously reaches across the table and takes a sip, raising the stakes in our father-daughter poker game. It's as though she were saying to me, *I* am *growing up, you know.* I assume it's legal for her to drink at eighteen in Quebec, and I begin to suggest that she order something if she wants it, but I lose my nerve.

We briefly discuss our interview tomorrow with Michael Greenfield, the reason we're in Montreal. I've dragged Sami along on my trip visiting guitar makers. Yesterday was Linda Manzer in Toronto, tomorrow is Michael Greenfield, Friday is Ken Parker, in New City outside of New York.

Our salads arrive, and the conversation turns, as it so often does these days, though always in a veiled way, to the unholy trinity of teenage life: boys, drugs, and alcohol. The sex lives of our children: now *there's* an undiscovered country. I'm not supposed to know half the things I know about Sami's life, and whenever we discuss these things she leaves out any scenes she thinks will meet with my disapproval, even though our conversation makes no sense without them.

For my part, I pretend to be too dumb and trusting to realize this.

It's hard to let your children grow up, I suppose. When Sami was smaller, I used to look at her and, with an exaggerated sense of wistfulness, say, "Do you *really* have to grow up?" until it occurred to me that, yes, she *has* to grow up, and the real question is: *Do I want her to have to do it knowing she's breaking her father's heart in the process?*

I'm aware of the dangers of naiveté. Still, I've begun to think that innocence is too often undersold. Yes, children must grow up, but no one wants his kid to be scorched by the fires of Love and Sex and by their ever-present hand-maidens, Rejection and Betrayal.

"True, true," Sami answers me philosophically when I say as much over dinner, "and that's why I think a person might want to . . . you know . . ."

"No, I don't know."

". . . experiment with a good friend," she says, locking a strand of hair behind her ear and taking a provisionary bite of her food.

"A person?" I say.

We're speaking in code again. Her boyfriend, Gideon, is back from a year in Israel—thanks to our trip visiting these luthiers, Samantha isn't there for his homecoming—and I gather that the two of them, best friends and occasionally girlfriend and boyfriend, are thinking about collaborating with each other in just such a spirit of experimentation and cooperation.

But as I say, I'm supposed to be too thick to interpret this code, and so I play along.

It's not up to me in any case. The girl's eighteen, nearly nineteen. She's given us practically no trouble as a teenager. Still, as though I were also speaking only theoretically, I suggest to her that *a person* might want to wait until he or she finds *another person* whom he or she really loves and who is also really loving.

"Preferably," I add—why not go for broke?—"within the constraints of the marriage vow."

The conversation goes back and forth like this. I'm aware that there are few societal norms to back me up. When Sami was in the eighth grade, her school brought in a psychologist to speak to the parents on the topic of sex and the middle-schooler. Her school was a community day school, a nominally religious school, but the psychologist, an older man with a white pompadour, seemed to have already thrown in the towel as far as the chastity of our children was concerned.

"But what can you do if you want your kid to get through high school *without* having sex?" I asked, raising my hand during the question-and-answer period.

I noticed a few of the fathers nodding their heads along with me.

"Ah! Oh?" The psychologist squinted in what seemed to be confusion. "*Without* having sex?" he said, as though this were the oddest question he'd ever in a lifetime of public speaking received.

"Yes, *without* having sex," I repeated.

"Oh, well then. I don't know." He chuckled. "Good luck with *that*." He shrugged. "Go work for Disney, I guess?"

MY OWN ATTEMPTS at first love were disastrous. I was a complete sexual maladroit. During my first year at college, I asked a woman from my French class out. Melanie was a little older than I was. I lived in a dorm, and she lived in a two-bedroom apartment off campus. That was the least of it. She also smoked and drank what I thought of as grown-up drinks. When I picked her up, for instance, she offered me a bourbon.

We went out to see a play, and when I brought her home, she invited me in, and though she was clearly flirting with me, sitting near me and laughing at my jokes, I was too shy to initiate a kiss. She was from Tennessee and perhaps too much of a good southern girl to make the first move.

She had no roommate, despite the second bedroom, and this was part of my confusion. When she walked me out to say good night, we stood in her doorway for a moment. Looking over her shoulder, I could see into her apartment. In the hallway behind her were the doors to both bedrooms, and when she lowered her eyes and asked me, "Would you like to stay the night?" the visual impression of these two doors was so overwhelming I presumed she meant in her spare bedroom, and because I was wearing my contact lenses, which in those days you couldn't sleep in, and because the bottle of saline solution and the little plastic case I kept them in were back in my dorm room, I said, "No, thanks, that's all right," and bid her good night.

I drove home, thinking nothing of it, happy to finally get my lenses out, happy to have had a pleasant-enough evening, and it was only during the summer following my freshman year—this was nine or ten months later—when

I was home for the summer break, walking around town and thinking about her, that it occurred to me what she had meant: *Would you like to stay the night?*

I couldn't believe it! I'd been propositioned for the first time in my life by an attractive woman, and to the offer of her body, to the offer of her love, to the offer of her sweet caresses, I had blithely answered, *No, thanks, that's all right.*

I stopped in my tracks. How could I have been so dense, so thick, so stupid?

Melanie and I had gone out a few other times, and now images from those dates came flooding back to me. I remembered sitting with her on her apartment floor, studying, her face buzzing around mine like a flower hoping to be pollinated by a bee, a bee too shy, too inattentive, too myopic, to cross the air between itself and the flower. *What if I'm misreading her signals?* I remember thinking. *How embarrassing would that be!*

But now, I saw clearly that—*of course! of course!*—she had been interested in *me*. I'd been blind to all the signs. In our French class, she'd even given me a birthday card. She'd written *"Je n'ai pas oublié"*—(I did not forget)—inside it, though the significance of this gesture was lost on me because I didn't know the verb *oublier*.

I vowed to redress this wrong. Returning to school in the fall, I immediately called her up. I still had her number, but I got one of those recorded messages saying the number you've dialed has been changed. The recorded voice gave me the new number. It was in an area code I didn't recognize, and when I called this new number, Melanie answered. I reminded her who I was, she seemed happy to hear from me, but dinner that night was out.

"What about tomorrow night then?"

"No, I can't. You see, I moved to Colorado over the summer, and I've enrolled in school here."

"In Colorado?"

"In Boulder, yeah."

It's not like I didn't have other options. Or at least one other option. It's not like I didn't have one other option. I had one other option. My high school girlfriend had followed me to college that year. Our relationship had been relatively chaste when I was a senior and she a junior in high school, but now things grew fractious between us as we tried, a year later, to reaccommodate each other into our newly adult lives. We were both virgins, and neither of us knew what we were doing. With my apartment mates out for the night, we spent an unhappy evening on the living room carpet with a pack of unlubricated condoms—these were cheaper than lubricated, and I assumed they did the job equally well—the light from the hallway spilling into the room.

Everything seemed scratchy: the condoms, the carpet, even the light, and Mary-Ann's small-town guilt-inflected evangelical abhorrence of sex only added to the coarse textures of the evening. Having, however imperfectly, surrendered her maidenhood to me, she hoped, I knew, that we would marry, the act of our marrying turning our nonmarital sex into premarital sex which, after our wedding, would become morally indistinguishable from marital sex.

I found marriage, as a concept, antiaphrodisiacal. Still technically a teenager, the expectation that I was somehow responsible for another person's happiness felt too burdensome to me, and we fell into a bad routine: as my ardor for Mary-Ann slackened, she'd gravitate towards another man, arousing my jealousy. My jealousy aroused, I'd woo her back, after which my ardor for her would slacken and she'd gravitate towards another man, thus rearousing my jealousy.

As time went on, the cycles of slackening ardor, gravitation towards other men, aroused jealousy, rewooing and reslackening grew shorter and shorter until they began to overlap. One night, having, I thought, successfully rewooed her, I left her room at her co-op only to feel my jealousy preternaturally aroused by the time I hit the street. Returning immediately, I pounded on her door. No one answered. I tried the knob. It was locked. Mary-Ann pretended, in the few minutes we'd been apart, to have fallen into a deep sleep. It took her ages to wake up and unlock her door, and then, as though we were all characters in a Noël Coward play, I searched her room and found her lover, the fellow from the room next to hers, hiding in her bathroom.

He'd slipped in as soon as he'd heard me leave.

The wear and tear on our hearts was exhausting us both. Our innocence in tatters, we raised the white flag of surrender, and Mary-Ann gravitated towards yet another man who had what the other other men she'd gravitated towards previously didn't have: a life in another city, to which he took her, far beyond the ambit of my rewooing.

I felt a sense of gratitude towards her new lover, and a year later, I was head over heels in love. Unlike Mary-Ann, Hedy was a sensualist, a feminine libertine, a lotharia, if such a term exists, with a long river of blonde hair running down her back. I was intoxicated by her, and miraculously she was drawn to me, although the feeling didn't remain mutual for long. Eight months into our relationship, I'd begun to suspect that Hedy was seeing someone else. Gravitation towards another man, slackening ardor—I knew all about that—although this time, the slackening ardor was hers for me, not mine for her. And as for rewooing, she'd been rewooed right out from under me.

Hedy had never mentioned another man, she'd never said anything at all. Still, I sensed his presence between us, and when I confronted her about it, she revealed that it was true. There was someone else. We had an enormous fight. Furious and heartbroken, I backed her into a corner of her apartment, demanding to know who she was seeing.

"Just tell me his name!" I shouted, and she spat the name—the name of her lover—into my face.

Oddly enough, it was my name.

An odd coincidence, I thought, though not a remarkable one. Mine is not an uncommon name, after all.

In any case, one way or the other, I was grimly satisfied. I had my answer: Hedy was seeing another man, another man named Joseph.

ALTHOUGH, AS IT turned out, she wasn't.

Months later, I was having a drink with my friend Jack. Jack had actually introduced Hedy and me, and they were still friends. So although I no longer had access to Hedy, I had access to Jack, and Jack had access to Hedy, and that was about as close as I was going to get to her.

"How's Hedy doing with this new boyfriend of hers, this Joseph?" I said, putting the question to Jack as casually as I could, dropping it into the conversation with as much insouciance as I could counterfeit, as though how the two of them were getting along, as well as the fact that Hedy had a new lover at all, was a matter of profound indifference to me, when, in truth, how Hedy and this new boyfriend of hers, this new Joseph, were doing was a question that obsessed me day and night, a subject I contemplated for hour upon miserable hour, sometimes while rolling on the floor of my room.

"Joseph?" Jack said, giving me a strange look.

I nodded, shrugging with an affected nonchalance.

"But *you're* Joseph," he said.

"Yes, I know, I'm Joseph, but—"

"No, I mean, you're *Hedy's* Joseph."

"Yes, I know. I'm Hedy's Joseph, but . . ."

"Although, of course, you're anything but Hedy's Joseph now."

". . . but isn't this new boyfriend of hers *also* named Joseph?"

"No. His name is David."

"David?"

"Yeah," Jack said.

"*David?*"

"David, yeah."

When I had demanded to know the name of Hedy's lover and she had shouted my own name back at me, something, I realized, must have been off in her intonation. She wasn't answering my question, as I had, for months, assumed. Rather, she was refusing to answer it, and in a state of emotional confusion, I had misunderstood her.

Now my humiliation was complete.

Is it any wonder then, not too long afterwards, when I met Barbara, the woman I eventually married, I fell upon her bosom—so to speak—like a castaway falling upon the shore?

I take a sip of my beer and look at Samantha, sitting across the table from me, blossoming out of the chrysalis of her adolescence into young womanhood.

Must I really send my only child out onto those same stormy seas?

WE RETURN, VIA the metro, to our hotel.

Once we're in the room, I check my email before getting into bed. Samantha stays up late, as she's done every night on this trip, binge-watching episodes of *Friends* on a Japanese bootleg video site.

In the middle of the night, I'm awakened by the sound of a woman achieving sexual climax.

I lift my head from the pillow, but I can't tell if it's coming from above or below us or from the room next door

The woman's voice is high, breathy, fluty. She gasps out a series of round, songlike, delirious tones—*Oh, Oh, Oh!*—that crescendo and stop, before beginning again and crescendoing again. I can't hear her partner. I assume she has one. I hope so anyway. It's a sweet sound, to tell you the truth, though I'm worried it has awoken Samantha and may be disturbing her as well.

SNIP SNIP SNIP

On our first date, Barbara told me her house was haunted. There was a ghost in her bedroom. Well, it wasn't her bedroom anymore. She moved all her stuff into the living room when the ghost showed up and sublet the bedroom to a park ranger who needed a place in town one weekend a month when he came out of the Kit Carson National Forest to visit his girlfriend.

I'd taken Barbara out for a Mexican dinner at the Taos Tennis Ranch.

I was only twenty-three. I'd dropped out of graduate school at the University of Chicago to spend a few months at an artist colony in Taos called the Helene Wurlitzer Foundation. I had dreams of becoming a great American playwright. I had no interest in becoming a great American, but I wanted to be a great American playwright, and the Wurlitzer Foundation provided me with time and a little adobe house in which to realize this dream.

Every morning at dawn, I made a pot of coffee, and dragging a table and a chair out onto the front porch, I wrote pages and pages of dialogue as the rising sun illuminated the dewy tips of the sagebrush and the magpies clattered in the trees.

Around eleven o'clock, I'd go into town for breakfast, and that's where I met Barbara. She was one of the owners of the Mainstreet Bakery, an all-natural bakery cafe that made twenty-one different kinds of whole wheat bread, which they sold locally and shipped throughout the Southwest and as far east as Chicago, which is where I would have been if I hadn't dropped out of graduate school.

There were actually three Barbaras at the bakery—Barbara Freer and Barbara Perrine owned the place, and Barbara Goldman worked for them—and they were all beautiful. I'd made a couple of friends at the Wurlitzer, a poet named Marea, a composer named Eric, and I entertained them with tales of my lovelorn life, recounting, really for their amusement alone, my heartsick oglings of the three Barbaras, these three muselike beings who moved with charm and grace through the bakery, taking orders, pouring coffee, sliding whole wheat pastries into refrigerated display cases, each more beautiful than the last.

I had no intention of asking any of the Barbaras out. I never spoke to them, in fact. My residency at the Wurlitzer was for three months, four at the most. There was no time for a relationship to go anywhere, and I was too busy becoming a great American playwright to be distracted by romance, and also, to be honest, too shy.

One evening, though, after Marea and Eric and I had spent the day hiking, we stopped by the bakery. The two of them started talking to one of the Barbaras, to Barbara Freer, as it turned out, the Barbara who would eventually become my Barbara. They were playing a kind of interpersonal poker game with me, chatting her up as she stood behind the cash register in her tank top and her white apron. They'd grown tired of my tales of passive longing, it seemed—a lesson for all writers: a passive protagonist frustrates an audience— and were taking matters into their own hands, pushing the story forward, raising the dramatic stakes, dive-bombing in like dare-devil pilots, almost revealing the truth of my infatuation to Barbara, before pulling back at the last possible moment.

"So, tell us, Barbara," Eric said, "with so many beautiful women working here, do you ever have problems with the male customers growing obsessed with them?"

"I imagine," Marea said, "that many, many customers develop deep crushes on the women who work here."

I was helpless to do or say anything. When Barbara wasn't looking, Marea and Eric flashed laughing, defiant faces at me, as though daring me to stop them—*One false move, buddy, one false move, and we'll reveal everything to her!*—in the meantime, finding out her name, telling her ours, and even inviting her to join us for dinner.

Luckily, she had plans that night and couldn't go out with us, but something had changed. A bridge had been crossed, and I found myself thinking exclusively about her and no longer about the other two Barbaras. Maybe I'd ask her out, after all. Thanks to Marea and Eric, we'd exchanged names, but I wanted to reinforce that information so that when I called her—I lacked the courage to approach her in person—she'd know who I was.

I began dropping little clues to my identity. As I was leaving the bakery one day, I asked her to throw away an envelope that was addressed to me, thinking she might glance at the address, as anyone might, see my name, and register it deep into her unconscious mind. I did a number of things like this—I don't remember what else—not yet knowing, since I didn't know her at all, that she wasn't the sort of person who noticed peripheral details.

And one night, believing the way had been prepared, I called her up.

The adobe houses the Wurlitzer Foundation provided

us had no phones—the better to seclude us from the outside world so we might concentrate on our imaginative work—and I walked to the town plaza to use a pay phone there. I found "Freer, B" in the phone book. In those days, women had begun listing their first names in the phone book by initial only, identifying themselves immediately, to perverts and crank callers, as women who lived alone, but frustrating the caller's ability, I guess, to address them by name. A net gain, I suppose. I dialed Barbara's number and she answered, and I immediately identified myself, demonstrating that I was neither a pervert nor a crank caller, but despite my weeks of careful preparation, it was clear she had no idea who I was.

I reminded her that we'd met when my friends and I came into her bakery and that I came into the bakery almost every day.

"A lot of people come into the bakery every day," she said. "Can you be more specific?"

I told her I got a bagel and coffee each time I was there.

"Oh, right!" she said. "You're the bagel man."

"I guess so. I don't know. Am I?"

"I was wondering if you were Greg Calbi's brother. *Are* you Greg Calbi's brother? Because you look very much like someone I grew up with."

No, I wasn't Greg Calbi's brother, I told her, but I *was* wondering if she'd like to go out to dinner with me sometime. She said she thought she might, and we agreed on a

day and an hour, and on that day and at that hour, I picked
her up and we drove to the restaurant at the Taos Tennis
Ranch, where, over enchiladas in mole sauce, she told me
about her ghost.

Now, you hear a lot of ghost stories in Taos. Everyone there seems to have lived in a haunted house at one
time or another. They've stumbled into their kitchens at 3
a.m. to find a group of ghostly miners playing poker there.
Or they have an uncle who shot a deer near the pueblo
only to discover, after tracking the animal down, that the
deer was a man who, laughing at his wounds, dissolved into
snow. Or they've heard luscious violin music coming from
an otherwise empty room.

Barbara's story included something rare in ghost stories,
she told me: third-person confirmation.

The house she lived in was a 150-year-old adobe house,
one in a row of such houses not far from the plaza. She
hadn't lived there very long. She'd moved in only the summer before. When, as a potential renter, she'd stopped by
to have a look, she liked everything about the house, except
one thing: the plastered walls of the bedroom were painted
a hot pink, and the vigas, the logs running the length of the
ceiling, were a sparkling metallic silver.

"I'll take it," she told the landlord, "if you'll paint the
room over in white."

"Agreed," the landlord said.

Barbara had heard that the tenant before her had killed himself in that room—"The paint job would have driven anyone to suicide," she told me—but this didn't dissuade her. The room repainted, she moved in, and a month or so later, when her sister Maureen came to visit, the two of them slept there together, in Barbara's big double bed, sleeping peacefully throughout Maureen's stay until the night they were awoken by the sound of a disembodied voice, chanting.

"What the *hell* is that?" Barbara said, sitting up in bed.

Maureen sat up as well.

They'd both heard it, a foreign-sounding voice chanting in a foreign language. The only word the two sisters recognized was *Zia*, the name of Barbara's Irish setter, who was lying at the foot of the bed. The voice had addressed the dog by name.

As abruptly as it started, it stopped, and the two sisters returned to sleep. They discussed it at breakfast, but nothing further happened, and neither of them thought much more about it. The summer ended. Maureen went home.

"And then," Barbara told me over our Mexican dinner, "I was lying in bed one morning, okay, and I get this really strong *hit* that I have to leave the room."

"A really strong *hit*?" I say.

"Yeah," she says, not realizing that I'm making fun of her. "But it was six o'clock in the morning, on a Sunday, right?, and there's no way I'm getting out of bed at that time. So

I turn over, I pull the covers up, okay, and that's when I hear it."

With the fingers of one hand, she mimes a scissors cutting over her head.

"*Snip snip snip,*" she says. "Very distinct, it's very distinctly the sound of a scissors snipping over my head." She raises her hands to her shoulders, palms outward, as though in surrender. "And I thought, *All right, all right, if that's how you feel about it, I'll go. I'll go. I'll leave the room.*"

She got up and made herself a cup of coffee, and she sat, drinking it, on the porch outside.

Sometime after that, she was having a drink with her business partner, Barbara Perrine, in the Taos Inn, when a woman Barbara Perrine knew came in. Barbara Perrine introduced her two friends, and the three women got to talking—you know: *Who are you? What do you do? Where do you live?*—when suddenly the third woman made the connection.

"Oh my God!" she said. "*You're* the one with the ghost!"

"Right, that's right," Barbara said. "I'm the one with the ghost."

"Oh, man!" the woman said. "You've got to tell me all about it. I knew that guy," she said. "I knew the guy that lived there, the guy that killed himself in that room. We were friends."

Barbara starts telling the woman the story. She tells her about the pink-and-silver bedroom.

"Yeah, yeah, right, right, that's right," the woman says. "I've *been* in that room."

Barbara tells her about how her sister came to visit and how the two of them were sleeping together in the room and how they were awoken in the middle of the night by a disembodied voice with a foreign accent, chanting in a foreign language, and how the only word she and Maureen could understand was the name of the dog, Zia, who the voice addressed by name.

"Oh, man," the woman said. "Whoa! All right."

Barbara told her how she'd been lying in bed at six o'clock on a Sunday morning and how she'd gotten a really strong hit to leave the room, but how, because it was only six in the morning, she'd rolled over and pulled the covers up, and how then she'd heard, very distinctly, above her head the sound of scissors snipping. Barbara mimes the scissors with her hand—*snip snip snip*—and the woman's face turns absolutely white.

"Oh my God!" she said. "That guy . . . the guy I knew . . . he was . . . that guy was a *dress* designer," she said. "He was from *Lebanon*. He was *Lebanese*," she said. "That room was his workroom, and he had literally *hundreds* of pairs of scissors hanging all over the walls in that room!"

"So that's proof, don't you think?" Barbara says, sitting across the table from me now.

"Proof?" I say.

"Yeah."

"Of what?"

"That ghosts exist."

This is not the direction I thought the story was taking.

"Yeah, I don't think so," I say, spearing my enchilada with a fork.

"What do you mean, you don't think so? That's third-person confirmation."

I was fresh out of college, more or less—I'd dropped out of graduate school at the University of Chicago, granted—and I considered myself an intellectual, a rationalist, a skeptic in the best sense of the word. And Barbara, I was beginning to realize, was a hippie chick, a flake, a real Taoseña.

I took a sip of my beer.

"Well," I say, "I mean, even if we accept the validity of this third-person confirmation of the experiences you claim to have had—if it even *is* third-person confirmation. I mean, isn't it really more like second-person confirmation? I mean, I'm not really willing to accept the ghost as a person—still, it really doesn't prove that the thing in your house was a ghost."

"What else could it have been then?" Barbara says. "The scissors, the foreign voice, the guy was a Lebanese dress-maker with scissors hanging all over the room!"

"I know, I know, but I'm just saying, logically . . . let's just say there *was* something there, okay, a disembodied *being* of some kind . . ."

"All right."

". . . who, let's say, exists . . . I don't know . . . beneath the threshold of our senses . . ."

"Okay."

". . . and for some reason, but for reasons we can't discern, this *being*, whatever it is, wants to make us believe in ghosts, all right?, then it wouldn't be a ghost."

"But that *is* a ghost."

"No, technically a ghost is the disembodied soul of a dead person who, for reasons we also don't understand, haunts this world, but the being I'm postulating was, let's say, never a person."

"What were they then?"

"I don't know, and that's my point. We don't know what they are."

"We don't know what they are, but they're not ghosts?"

"Exactly."

"But for some reason they want to make us believe in ghosts?"

"Theoretically, I'm saying."

"And for some reason, if I'm understanding you correctly, these beings who, cross-culturally, all across the world, are not ghosts, have somehow convinced us all that there *are* ghosts?"

"Again, only theoretically."

"And you can believe in the existence of these beings, but you don't believe in ghosts?"

"No, I don't believe in these beings," I say. "All I'm saying is that the possibility that such beings exist is enough to rule out the existence of a ghost in your house."

Barbara looks around the restaurant, as though searching for help. "But we don't even have a *word* for these things you're talking about."

"I know."

"Even though *everybody* everywhere in the world knows about ghosts."

"Which is perhaps a measure of how good these things, whatever they are, are at what they do."

"I had a ghost," Barbara says.

"If you want to think so, okay."

"There was something there. I mean, Earthrise and his girlfriend even held a cedar burning in that room."

"Earthrise?"

"The park ranger I sublet the room to. That's how Native Americans smoke out an unhappy spirit."

"Yeah?"

"By burning cedar, but nothing seemed to work."

I HATE TO sound superficial—although, of course, I was twenty-three; I *was* superficial—but I'd begun writing Barbara off from the moment I picked her up. Zia had jumped all over me when I came into her house, and Barbara turned out to be one of those people who speak to their animals in high silly voices. She was wearing a red velvet vest with a matching skirt that I didn't find attractive. We'd been awkward with each other the entire evening, and now this crazy ghost story. I didn't believe in ghosts. I didn't believe in astrology or astral projection. I didn't believe in healing crystals or Tarot cards or the thousand and one other mystical disciplines the Taoseños I'd been meeting seemed to have staked their lives on, devoting years and incalculable trust fund dollars, hard-earned by someone if not by themselves, towards mastering.

It all seemed ridiculous to me, self-deluded, credulous, pathetic, and long before our dinner ended, I knew I'd never ask Barbara out again.

The only problem was: this meant not going into the bakery. I avoided it for a week, though I doubt Barbara even noticed. I suspect she hadn't had much of a good time either. I mentioned none of this to Marea and Eric. I stopped spinning my lovelorn tales for their amusement and tried to concentrate on becoming a great American playwright again, getting up before dawn, sitting on my porch with a cup of coffee, sketching out scenes, while the magpies chattered in the trees.

Finally, though, I couldn't take it anymore. The food was too good, and I missed the gentle hippie vibe of the place. It was a public establishment, I told myself. Nothing prevented me from going there. Maybe Barbara wouldn't even be in. Or maybe, busy in the back, she wouldn't even see me.

When I entered, though, she was standing behind the front counter, in her tank top and her white apron, placing a stand of freshly baked Ischler Tortelettes beneath a glass display dome.

"Hello, my friend," she said, reaching across the counter to shake my hand. "I haven't seen you in a while."

"I've been out of town," I told her.

She offered me a cup of coffee and invited me into the back so she could keep working while we talked. It was late in the afternoon, and things were slow. The bread bakers hadn't begun prepping for the night. Most of the waiters and the lunch cook had gone home. The big delivery door in the back was wide open, and through it, the intense afternoon sun lit up a Rothko-like rectangle of orange adobe wall.

I sat on a high stool, sipping my coffee, watching Barbara ice a lemon poppy seed cake. I admired her unhurried quickness and her skill. Our conversation seemed easier. Maybe we were like war buddies—we'd been through a horrendous experience, our date, together—or like soldiers who'd fought and survived in opposing armies and who, after the battle, discover how much they have in common now that nothing is at stake; maybe it was the scent of cinnamon and chocolate and honey in the air, or maybe it was the sense of home a merchant's son feels being in the back of a store, but I found myself enjoying her company.

In addition to her inattention to peripheral detail, Barbara possessed another quality I was unaware of at the time: a highly articulated sense of fair play. Though neither of us had enjoyed our night out I *had* bought her dinner, and now she felt she owed me a meal. She invited me over for breakfast that Saturday, after which, I'm sure she was thinking, we'd be even and she'd never have to see me again.

I ARRIVED AT her house a little before nine. She'd made a delicious meal: homemade buckwheat pancakes with fresh maple syrup, yogurt and wild strawberries picked in the Rio Grande gorge. Afterwards, we sat on her couch, in front of a small fire, talking easily about everything, it seemed: our childhoods, old lovers, the music we listened to, the books that had touched us, my ambitions as a writer, her hopes for the bakery.

Around noon, she excused herself to make a phone call. She returned to the couch, where we kept talking until five, at which point she told me that, as unusual as it was for her, she had three dates scheduled for the day: a breakfast date with me, a lunch date with another guy, and a dinner date with an architect who had built his own house, bermed into the mountainside.

She'd canceled the lunch—that's what the noontime call had been about—but the architect was cooking and there was no way she was missing out on a meal prepared for her by someone else.

But we began seeing each other regularly after that.

• • •

Now, as skeptical as I'd been about Barbara's ghost, not long afterward the house began to fall apart. The electricity shorted out constantly, the pipes beneath the house burst, the basement flooded, the oven worked only erratically. Befuddled repairmen came and went, conferring with one another in Spanish, and no one could figure out what the matter was.

Even Earthrise and his girlfriend decamped, driven out by the bad vibes.

And eventually Barbara moved out as well.

Long after we were married, years after we'd moved away, Barbara and I came back to Taos. We stopped by the house and saw that it was boarded up; and the next time we returned, a few years after that, it had been torn down. The space where the house had been, this space in a line of adobe houses, looked like a gap in a row of teeth. It made no sense. Who tears down a 150-year-old adobe house half a block from the plaza?

As the years passed, I had my share of unworldly experiences. One night, it rained *inside* my sister's apartment while I was sleeping on her couch. This wasn't a dream. The rain woke me up, and it had come in answer to a theological question I had posed. Another time, my car, my *actual* car, was stolen after I'd promised it to a trio of women I'd encountered in a dream. Once, I found the title of a screenplay I'd written in a novel I'd never read. (The screenplay was called "The Richardson-Murchison Wedding"; and in Evan S. Connell's *Mr. Bridge*, Mr. Bridge asks his secretary to bring him the Richardson-Murchison file.)

True, I never encountered Barbara's ghost, but there was another unworldly presence in that old adobe house. It wasn't an angry spirit from the past, but a benevolent soul from my future. Sitting with Barbara that day on her couch, talking from dawn until dusk, it felt as though we'd known each other our entire lives, and as it's turned out, we more or less have.

PAUL MCCARTNEY'S PHONE NUMBER

It was the end of 1989, and I was walking through the parking lot at LAX. I don't recall where I was going, but I was traveling alone, and I noticed a slip of paper on the ground. Someone had neatly written the name Paul McCartney on it, above a local phone number.

I couldn't believe it! I'd found Paul McCartney's phone number! I scooped the paper up and put it in my pocket. I had time before my flight, so I thought I'd call the number just to hear who answered, just to—perhaps—hear Paul McCartney's voice on the line, that all-too-familiar Liverpudlian voice, saying hello.

Or maybe Ringo, sitting by the phone, would answer it.

I dropped my quarter into the slot. My hand trembled as I punched in the number. The phone rang a couple of times. I held my breath. Finally, a woman answered.

"Ticketmaster," she said. "May I help you?"

IRVIN IN
WONDERLAND

I went to Oklahoma City to see my father. This was after he'd woken up from his coma but was still in the hospital. The elevator doors glided open on his floor, and his wife was standing on the other side in a bright yellow pantsuit. I was never sure, whenever we met, how she'd treat me. For years, I could barely get a "good morning" out of her. She was the sort of person who could come into a room and say "good morning" to everyone but one person, and that person was usually me. Lately, she'd warmed up a bit—I have no idea why—and now, as we encountered each other across the undulating threshold of the elevator, she seemed happy, relieved even, to see me, although *relieved* in the military sense is probably the correct word: as soon as I arrived for hospital duty, she abandoned the post and, though I spent almost every hour in my father's room for the next week and a half, I never saw her again during my stay.

I was surprised by her friendliness and the rush of enthusiasm in her voice. "Thank goodness you're here!" she said, leading me to a small sitting area not far from the bank of elevators. "I have *no idea* what to do with your father."

"Really? What's the matter?"

She huffed out a short breath. "Well, he's been having visions . . ."

"Visions?"

". . . or hallucinations or I don't *know* what all, and he's been saying the oddest things."

"Yeah? What kind of things?"

"Well, he's been seeing—oh, well, I don't know—but *animals* moving through the walls, and he wants to know if they're real or not, and I just don't know what to tell him."

"C'MERE," MY FATHER said when I entered his room. He was lying in his hospital bed, in a gown. "No, here," he said with an intensity I wasn't used to meeting in his gaze. "Sit right across from me." Extending his arm, he reached for my hand. "So that we can speak *panim el panim*."

Panim el panim?

Now, this was weird in a thousand different ways. To begin with, my father wasn't an overtly religious man. His life centered on business, on golf, on his membership in the Masonic Temple. He had not, to my knowledge, ever delved into the Torah, nor had he lived in a community whose members delved into the Torah. Even his rabbi, I'm sure, had probably never delved too deeply into the Torah, nor—I'm certain of this—had my father ever spoken a word of conversational Hebrew in his life. In the Reform synagogue of my childhood, even the Sh'ma, the affirmation of God's oneness, was recited in English—and yet, here he was, addressing me in the Hebrew of the Bible, quoting Exodus 33:11, to be exact: "And the Holy One spoke to Moses face-to-face—*panim el panim*—as one man speaks to another."

Weirder still was hearing him do so in his thick West Texas accent, its vowels bent out of shape like nails yanked out of a piece of wood: *pan-eye-yim ale pan-eye-yim.*

Dad's stay in the hospital lasted exactly sixty days. Oddly enough, he'd been admitted on Tisha B'Av, perhaps the darkest day on the Hebrew calendar, a day of wailing and mourning, commemorating the destruction of the ancient temple in Jerusalem, and he would be released the day after Yom Kippur, the Day of Atonement.

According to mystical tradition, this period is freighted

with meaning. Between the "black fast" of Tisha B'Av and the "white fast" of Yom Kippur, introspection and repentance are the order of the day.

Dad grasped my hands and pulled me closer to him. There were some things he wished to discuss with me, he said, family things and the like, this bad blood between me and his wife, et cetera, et cetera, and as we talked, holding on to each other's hands, our conversation slid down many other avenues, and he began to obsess over why he'd been given, as he put it, "this extra time."

This seemed an odd way of thinking to me.

"We're given whatever time we're given, Dad. Why think of any of it as *extra*?"

But no, he seemed convinced of it, and as though one thing had to do with the other, he sat up on the side of his bed and began telling me about his recent experiences.

"The Shriners had taken me to New York, to a hotel in New York," he said. "And they'd brought along this girl, a girl I was supposed to marry."

"A girl?"

He nodded. "It'd all been arranged."

"Okay."

"And what I don't understand is . . ."

"Yeah?"

"Did I *dream* it? Am I *remembering* it? Or did it actually *happen*?"

He scratched his scalp through the coils of his gray-black hair, and we were quiet for a moment. I was, by this time, sitting next to him on the bed, massaging his shoulders and his neck, something he loved for me to do.

"And did you know this woman, Dad?"

He shook his head, his wide neck moving beneath my hand.

"I mean, did you recognize her?"

"I'd never *seen* her before in my life!" he exclaimed, sounding as though the woman in question had accused him of a crime.

"And . . . and what was the *feeling* of the experience?"

He cocked his ear towards me. "The feeling?"

"Yeah."

"What do you mean, the feeling?"

"Yeah, I mean, what did it feel like?"

"Really good," he said, having thought it over. "It felt really good."

This had been after he'd gone into his coma, after the machines he was attached to in the ICU went kablooey, after the Code Blue had been sounded and the chaplain in her boxy skirt set had come into his room and asked if she could sit with us. I had that afternoon filled out a Do Not Resuscitate order for him. My brother and sisters had stood around his bed, and as his elder son, I had recited Vidui, the deathbed confession, on his behalf. Later, as he lingered in the coma, I'd sit near his bed and look into his face, which at times—there's no other way to describe it—seemed to be radiating light.

I told him all this as we sat together now on his hospital bed. I know a bit about Jewish mysticism, about the *mysterium coniunctionis* between Tiferet and Malchut in the Garden of Pomegranates, the divine marriage between the male and the female halves of the cosmos, and I suggested to my father, clearly now in an altered state, that perhaps at some point during his coma his soul might have been elsewhere than firmly locked within the prison house of his body, stretched, as it were, to the ends of its elastic, and that the wedding his fellow Shriners made for him might have actually occurred, although in a place with fewer than four dimensions.

This was not the kind of conversation I usually had with my father, and yet against all expectations, the answer seemed to satisfy him. His restless probing of the incident ceased, and he seemed pleased not to have to dismiss his dream-bride as a figment of his imagination.

WE SPENT DAYS together with him in this state. It lasted the entire time I was there. Later, a nurse told me that thanks to the deficiencies in his kidney function, the lip balm they'd given him for a fever blister had caused him to hallucinate. At the time, though, all I knew was that he seemed to have dropped a very potent tab of acid. Lying in his bed, he'd see things flying through the walls. "*Fligl*," he'd say, "little wings" in Yiddish, giggling like a child and nodding at me with a sort of conspiratorial nod.

Hurricane Katrina was on its way, and with newscasts unspooling endlessly into his room through the TV mounted on the wall, Dad became preoccupied with the story. One day, looking troubled, he said to me, "Now, if we can't live on the land, and if we can't live in the sea, then where *are* we going to live?"

Before I could address his mad concerns, a nurse entered the room, an African woman whose coal-black face seemed radiant and glowing. I thought Dad might lose his train of thought amid all the nursely commotion, but the question seemed too vital for him, too pressing.

"I know!" he said ten minutes later, snapping his fingers, as though he'd solved an abstruse mathematical equation.

"Yeah, Dad? What is it?"

"We can all live in Hyperspace!"

He grinned at me, lit up, like the Cheshire Cat. I didn't know how to answer him. I didn't know how what to say. This was not the father I remembered, the father who spent his mornings in retirement selling stock options, the father who, in a foreign city, preferred sitting in his hotel room to walking the streets, a man with no patience for philosophical speculations. That my father might use a word like *hyperspace* seemed as strange to me as had his speaking in Hebrew.

"Do you *see*?" he said to me now, lowering his voice.

"See what, Dad?"

"*Look!*" he whispered urgently.

"Okay, Dad, but what am I looking at?" I said, whispering as well.

"At the *nurse!*" he said, lowering his voice even further, gesturing discreetly towards her with his chin.

"Okay? Yeah?"

"Isn't it obvious?" he said.

"Isn't what obvious, Dad?"

"That *she's* been swimming in Hyperspace!"

I looked at the nurse, and perhaps because of her tranquil expression and her graceful presence and the calm with which she seemed to be taking in the world around her, I sort of understood—no, I understood exactly what my father meant. By this time, *I* had verses of Song of Songs rolling through my head: *Turn back, turn back, O Shulamit, that we may gaze upon you!*

Ever the gentleman, Dad pulled me closer. "You don't think I've offended her by saying that, do you?"

I looked at the nurse again, at her face as radiant and tranquil as the night sky.

"No, I don't think so, Dad."

"Good."

He nodded, reassured.

DAYS PASSED, AND though I admit I enjoyed my father's company in this state—we had never, in fact, gotten along so well—the experience was exhausting. It was like keeping up with a brilliant child who, obsessed with the subtleties of quantum physics, refuses to take a nap.

"Take a note!" he said one day, rocketing up straight in his hospital bed, the tails of his gown flying. I grabbed my notepad and my pen. "This is for the will!"

We had agreed, before I arrived, that together we'd write his ethical will, a document for subsequent generations. At last, he seemed ready to begin. "I sired Israel!" he exclaimed, dictating to me. "Twelve tribes, and a portion for each tribe, and a double portion for Ethan"—my brother—"being gay."

Naturally, I was concerned for his well-being. What *were* these hallucinations? How worried should I be about them? Were they part of some larger medical issue? And so periodically, although a bit reluctantly—we'd never had so much fun together—I'd call in a nurse, and acting the concerned son, I'd say, "See here now . . . I think my father here . . . well, I think he might be hallucinating."

"Hallucinatin'?" the nurse, whoever she was, and there were many of them during the course of my stay, said each time, and always, it seemed to me, with an unwarranted dose of skepticism.

"I think so, yeah. A little bit, I mean."

"Hm."

Each time, the nurse leaned over my father's bed. She'd put her face into his, and in a High Plains accent, with vowels as wide as open barn doors, she'd shout: "Mr. Skaw-bail, hew's the prezidaint of the Yew-Knotted Staites?"

Dad would tell her, and then she'd say, "N dew yew gnaw whot dye is it todye?"

None of the nurses seemed to mind that, before answering this question, Dad always turned and checked the digital calendar clock hanging on the wall near his bed. I suppose it seemed a rational thing to do.

"N dew yew gnaw whar yew R?"

Sometimes Dad would make a complicated Texas joke, telling the nurse that he was in plain view—Plainview being a small town outside of Lubbock—meaning, of course, that he was right in front of her, but since he wasn't in Lubbock, but in Oklahoma City, I'd have to explain the joke, a joke that indicated that perhaps Dad didn't actually know where he was, after all, a point that seemed to get lost in the tangle of humor, and then the nurse would always turn to me and shrug. "Sames awl wrought t' may."

"You're listening to the heart of the Republican Party," Dad told one nurse, when she'd placed a stethoscope on his chest.

"Is that wrought?"

"Yes, ma'am."

"Sames awl wrought t' may," the nurse said, shrugging, the stethoscope still in her ears. This time, though, when the nurse shrugged and said, "Sames awl wrought t' may," I told her, "Yeah, yeah, well, okay, I mean, he can answer all those questions—although he did look at the calendar clock for the second one—but you see that nurse right there?" I pointed towards the beautiful Shulamit who had, in the meantime, come back into our room. "Well, a moment ago, my father told me that he could tell that she had been swimming in Hyperspace, okay?"

The nurse took this in.

"In High-per spice?"

"In Hyperspace, yes," I said, "yeah."

"Daid he?" she asked her dark-skinned colleague. My word alone was insufficiently credible, it seemed. The beautiful nurse nodded, affirming my statement, her face as tranquil as ever.

"Ah, whale then," the other nurse said, "I gaz we better do sumpen 'bout it then."

It took days for Dad to come down off his high, days and nights during which we continued our Irvin in Wonderland explorations of consciousness and meaning.

"Did a rabbi come in with you yesterday?" he asked me at one point.

"No, Dad. Why?"

"Oh, well, I thought I saw a little guy in a black suit and a beard look in the doorway right after you arrived."

Another mystical vision, I assumed, but a day later a man

fitting that exact description entered our room, introducing himself not as a rabbi but as a minister. Another one of the hospital chaplains, he and my father began chatting away like old friends—Dad was always good with people—and when Dad learned that the chaplain, though born in Honduras, had been to seminary in Germany, he began speaking German with him.

More or less fluently, it seemed to me.

Which was odd, because I'd never heard my father speaking German before.

IT MAKES YOU wonder: How much of ourselves do we really know? How much of ourselves do we hide, even from ourselves, behind the masks we wear? The lip balm had cleansed the doors of perception for my father, but which was the real man, the stern, straight-laced paterfamilias I'd known my entire life or the cosmic cowboy, this blissful rider of the Purple Haze, tumbling along with the tumbling tumbleweeds of ecstatic consciousness through the fragrant bowers of the Garden of Pomegranates to a hotel in New York City where, radiant as a bride on her wedding day, his soul was trembling in anticipation of his arrival?

"What am I *doing*?" Dad said once into the phone when his brother Richard called him. "Joseph and I are talking about things that you could never understand because you're just too much of a dipstick!"

The truth is: he hadn't been the easiest of fathers. I was always a little bit afraid of him when I was a kid. He had an unpredictable temper and you never knew when you might set him off and find yourself the object of his wrath. At six foot two, he towered over us, and when he was angry, he'd set upon you with all the fury of an indignant prosecutor, his voice a booming, aggrieved growl. As an adolescent, my very presence seemed to irritate him. My hair was too long, my politics too liberal, my ambitions too unworldly. As I grew older, he seemed to place himself between me and everything that mattered to me. There were some very bad moments between us, which we never discussed or resolved, and as a consequence of this—or who knows why?—we never really developed a sense of intimacy. I never learned to speak truthfully to him. I never felt at ease in his presence, and whenever we were together we tended to hide from each other behind our careful masks.

And so I was grateful that Dad's visionary trip coincided with my visit, and I was probably the only member of the family who could have entered into this alternate universe with him and rolled. My sister Cindy, for instance, coming on duty not long after I left, overheard Dad on the phone describing to a cousin how he'd come to be in the hospital. "It's the strangest thing," he said. "I was standing in front of a dual-prop plane when one of the propellers somehow lopped off my leg!"

Cindy went immediately to his bedside, and pulling back his covers, she demonstrated to him the irrefutable evidence of his two legs lying, visibly intact, before him.

"Damn!" was all he could say.

Cindy told me, "I'd been wondering why, at physical therapy that morning, he kept saying to his therapist, 'Not bad for a one-legged man!'"

The psilocybinic lip balm had somehow liberated us both. The polite, wary distance between us seemed to collapse in on itself. Dad seemed funny and free, and for the first time, we seemed to be speaking a common language. For the first time, we seemed to be speaking to each other face-to-face, *panim el panim*, and for a while, even after the nurses resolved the issue and proscribed the lip balm, this increased sense of intimacy, this deeper knowing of each other continued. It resonated in our long-distance phone calls where the affection between us was palpable in a way it had never been.

"*When* are you coming back?" Dad said whenever I phoned. "I really want to *see* you again."

But then, of course, time passed. The Garden of Pomegranates receded in the distance, the little winged creatures stopped flying through the walls, the air no longer crackled with verses from the Song of Songs, Katrina devastated New Orleans, and no one sought refuge in Hyperspace, the German and Hebrew words fell out of Dad's conversation, his missing leg returned, he forgot all about the wedding in New York, the sixty days between Tisha B'Av and Yom Kippur fell off the calendar like leaves falling off a tree, and Dad, released from the hospital, returned to his normal state of consciousness.

Out of long habit, our old masks were restored. He and I returned to our old guarded positions, and the next time I saw him we were distant and correct with each other once again.

GET YOUR FEET BACK ON THE GROUND

I was standing in the lobby of the Südbahnhof in Vienna, waiting for Barbara. She'd stepped into the restroom to freshen up. It was a bright and ringing morning, the early light had a sparkling, crystalline quality to it as it poured through the glass walls of the station.

We were catching a train to Prague.

I was staring into space, entranced by the movement of people around me, and slowly I became aware that I was tapping out a rhythm on my teeth—an activity my dentist has continually warned me against—while a song played in my head.

I could hear a voice, in my inner ear, singing about living a little and being a gypsy and getting around with your feet back on the ground. Though these four bars of music go through my head periodically, I couldn't remember where they were from at first, though I was certain they were being sung by Paul McCartney. I can hear his round-toned falsetto perfectly on my mental hi-fi, but is it from *Band on the Run*? Or *Wild Life*? These are albums I no longer listen to.

No, I realize, it's a bit of Beatley nonsense from the end of a song called "Uncle Albert/Admiral Halsey" on the album *Ram*.

I find the whole thing depressing. I'm forty-four, and I can barely bring to mind the sound of my mother's voice. She's been gone now for nearly twenty years. I can remember nothing of my high school Spanish and next to nothing of my college French. I had a hard time recently remembering an entire trip Barbara and I made to England. I can't for the life of me remember the name of two women I was absolutely smitten with in college. I've forgotten entire episodes from every epoch of my life. There are people I was once close to who I might not recognize if I passed them on the street.

But somehow this piece of aural bubblegum, this pop nursery rhyme, this scatted little bit of Mother-Gooserai, which I heard for the first time nearly thirty-one years ago, plays faithfully in my head, probably—if the musicologists are to be believed—in the right key and at the right tempo, no matter where I am, even in a train station half a world away from home.

Paul McCartney probably doesn't even remember these four bars—they sound like something he improvised in the studio—but I'll be humming them, I know, for the rest of my life and probably on my deathbed, when I can remember nothing else, my teeth worn down to their nubs.

ABSOLUTE ELSEWHERE

A riot of blue and red filled the interior of my car, pulsating against the dashboard. By the time I pulled over and rolled down my window, the cop was already standing there.

"Your registration is expired," he said.

"Expired?"

"And I'm afraid that's an offence I have to impound your car for. Please step out of your vehicle, sir."

I was only twenty-four, and though I'd been living in Taos for a couple of years, I still had Texas plates. By reflex, I moved to get out of the car—it would never have occurred to me to disobey a policeman—but then I thought about how disagreeable getting home was going to be, not to mention the bureaucratic hassle of getting my car returned the following day.

"Really?" I said, sliding back into my seat. "You have to impound the car? I mean, isn't that a little drastic?"

"Okay," the cop said, "I won't impound the car, but I have to give you a ticket, and these tickets can be very expensive, probably like a hundred dollars."

"A hundred dollars?" I said.

He nodded. He was a tall, skinny Spanish guy.

"Really?" I said.

"Yes, sir."

In 1984, my monthly rent for the house I shared with Barbara in Arroyo Hondo was only ninety-seven dollars.

"Isn't that a little steep?"

Mild protest had worked the first time. *Why not,* I thought, *go for broke?*

"Steep?" the cop said.

"I mean, don't you think?"

"Well, there's nothing I can do about that," he said.

"Okay," I said.

"But here's the mayor's name and his phone number."

He wrote the name Floyd Montoya on the back of the ticket, along with a telephone number.

"Floyd Montoya?" I said.

"You can call Floyd. This is his home number." He turned his wrist and looked at his watch. "It's only ten. He's probably still up."

"This is the mayor's number?"

"His home phone, yeah." The cop smiled unhappily. "I mean. He's the only one that can do anything about the fine."

TAOS, I HAVE to say, wasn't like the rest of America. It wasn't like any place I'd ever lived. Even in the Reagan eighties, long after the hippies surrendered their hold on it, Taos was absolute elsewhere, not quite Mexico, but not really the States. You could feel it as soon as you crossed the Texas border: you were someplace else, your feet, high up—over seven thousand feet—in the mountains, your head higher up still in the thin desert air. The place was like a Sandplay therapist's toy box, filled with Jungian archetypes: artists, swamis, gurus, cowboys, Indians, satyrs. I knew a woman who lived in a chicken coop with her three young children. I knew a guy who played his wooden flute all day by the Rio Grande. Victor, a white-haired poet, sold his poems out of a little box under the eaves of the plaza, while Miles, a silent guy with a blond Prince Valiant haircut, practiced tai chi with a wooden sword every morning in the plaza's gazebo, his muscular thighs bulging in tight

tight shorts, no matter how cold it was. Everything in Taos was slightly askew. There was even a mime called Klein the Mime who talked during his act.

The culture was tripartite: the Anglos controlled the money, the Spanish ran the government, while the Indians worked the spirit of the place.

It wasn't for everyone. Taos Mountain, according to the locals, either accepted or rejected you.

I looked down at the ticket in my hand and read the name again: Floyd Montoya. Floyd Montoya was a barber with a shop right on the plaza. I could see it from where the cop and I were standing. The words FLOYD MONTOYA, OWNER, were painted in red on the white-washed adobe wall next to the door. Despite the cop's urging, I didn't feel I could call the mayor at home in the middle of the night and ask him to reduce my traffic fine.

Instead, the next morning I called my father.

In those days, the family business took care of everything, including our car registrations. For a while even, until the IRS closed the loophole, we all paid for our gas with company credit cards.

Dad transferred the call to Dorothy, his office manager. She'd renew the registration, she told me, and send me the tags later that day.

The next week, I went to the town hall for what I suppose was my trial. I found the correct office. A long narrow room, it had nothing in it but a desk and two chairs. A woman sat behind the desk. A man stood behind her chair. The woman was slender, middle-aged, with a helmet of bluntly cut hair. She wore a simple plaid cotton shirt. She squinted one eye against the smoke of a cigarette. The man was squat with a pointed belly, a salt-and-pepper crew cut, and an Errol Flynn mustache.

I'd never seen the woman before, but the man looked familiar. Later, I realized he was the chief of police, but that day, because he wasn't in uniform, I couldn't quite place him.

Like the cop, they were both Spanish.

I took a seat on the far side of the desk. They asked me what I was doing there. I told them I'd been driving with an expired registration, and I handed them my ticket and the new registration forms.

"Why were you driving with an expired registration?" the woman asked.

"Oh. Well, it was in the mail," I said. "The registration. It got delayed in the mail."

"Ah, it was in the mail," the police chief said, as though this explained everything. "It was in the mail," he said to the woman.

"It was in the mail?" she said to me.

"It was in the mail," I said, "yeah."

She looked over the paperwork again, the cigarette burning between her lips.

"But here it says you got the ticket on the twenty-first,

and according to this, the registration wasn't purchased until the twenty-second.

"Hmm," the police chief said, reading over her shoulder.

They both looked at me. I felt a moment of visceral panic. My breathing constricted. While keeping as bland a face as possible, I riffled through my brain for an additional lie that might make my first lie appear true.

"Well, I *thought* it was in the mail" was all I could come up with.

"Oh, you thought it was in the mail?" the police chief said.

We nodded at each other.

"He *thought* it was in the mail," the police chief said to the woman.

"You *thought* it was in the mail?" she said to me, sounding dubious, annoyed, it seemed to me, by the masculine collusion in the room.

"Yeah, I mean, I *thought* it was in the mail," I said.

She read through the papers again, frowning, comparing the ticket and the registration form.

"Well, *normally*," she finally said, "this ticket has an eighty-dollar fine, but since you *thought* the registration was in the mail, I'm only going to charge you twenty."

The police chief shrugged apologetically.

"Fair enough," I said.

I wrote out a check for twenty dollars and gave it to the

woman. She thanked me, I thanked her. I shook hands with the police chief and I walked down the rickety wooden staircase and out of the building into the bright morning light of the plaza, thinking maybe, just maybe, the Mountain had accepted me.

DON'T MESS WITH MISTER IN BETWEEN

My uncle Ike had had a rough couple of years, and I was worried about him. My mother's kid brother, he'd been largely abandoned by my sisters, both of whom lived less than a mile from his apartment. They'd given our father, in the last years of his life, the sort of attention a dying king might receive—his every need attended to during a full roster of daily visits—but for my uncle, it was different. Though my brothers-in-law saw to his financial and medical needs, as far as company went, Ike was on his own. I'm not blaming my sisters. Ike had, in fact, shunned *them*, partly as a result of mental instability, I think, and partly in order to more freely indulge his recreational drug habit.

Unbeknownst to almost everyone in the family, he'd struggled with addiction most of his life and had been using now for years. When he went through a quarter of a million dollars' worth of crack, we had to sell his sister's condo in Chicago, which he'd inherited, and move him to a small apartment in Dallas, where we could keep a better eye on him.

For an addict, he was an exemplary fellow: he never stole from anyone; he never hit anyone up for cash. At the first of the month, when his VA and his Social Security checks arrived, he simply took the bus and the DART to wherever addicts go in Dallas and used a portion of the money, dedicated to that purpose, for crack. This was the A-Side of his life, the hit side. It lasted about two weeks each month. When the money was gone, he returned to his apartment for the B-Side, doing whatever it was he did—sitting quietly for the most part and watching television—while waiting for our government to further finance his addiction.

Despite his using, he was the longest-living member of his family. His parents and his sisters—my aunt and my mother—had predeceased him, and he was older now than any of them had been at the time of their deaths. Lately, though, illness had caught up with him, and he'd been forced to abandoned his *hobby*. This was his cheerful code

word for his drug use. The shortness of breath caused by his
COPD made inhaling crack, he told me, a complete waste
of time and money.

I DECIDED TO go see him, and as I was packing for
my flight, I noticed a set of CDs on my bookshelf, a collection of lectures I'd bought years before on various aspects
of "Jewish healing." These were basically modern rabbinic
takes on ancient Jewish rituals. I'd listened to only a few of
these lectures. The CDs had been sitting on my shelf for
years. On impulse now, I downloaded one of the lectures to
my iTunes and uploaded it to my iPod and sipping a spicy
tomato juice high above the clouds, I listened to the first
half of it on my flight.

The subject was the annulment of vows. The lecturer
was a rabbi named Tirzeh Firestone. On the CD, Rabbi
Firestone calls the rabbinic ritual for the annulment of vows
"an ancient form of Judaic medicine" designed to "free the
captive soul" from the oaths it has made.

The ancients, she said, understood the powerful connection between breath, word, and intention, and as a consequence, they took the making of oaths very seriously. In the
modern world, we've lost touch with the idea that our words
might hold power over our lives. In the material world,
words seem the least material of things, and it's hard for us
to believe that making a vow might affect our destinies.

On the other hand, though our thoughts are even *less*

physical, we hold a profound respect for the power of the unconscious mind, and we know that a person might harbor a deep thought, unknown even to his rational, daylit self, that might constrict, inhibit, or imprison him.

Rabbi Tirzeh tells the story of a boy who developed leukemia at the age of sixteen and who fervently prayed, in his youthful naiveté, to be allowed to live until sixty. The boy recovered, and the man he became forgot all about his illness, until he was sixty and it returned. She describes a woman who, in the thrall of childbirth, screamed out, "I will never bear another child!" and who, ten years later, doesn't understand why she can't conceive a second time.

All this made sense to me. I knew a woman who, in the wake of her breast cancer, prayed to live to see her grandchildren. Her cancer, fatal this time, returned twenty years later, once her grandchildren had all been born.

According to Tirzeh, although we no longer make public vows, our unconscious intentions, these deep promises that, speaking aloud, we make to ourselves, continue to hold us in their sway.

MIDWAY THROUGH THE lecture, my plane began its descent. I wrapped the iBuds around my iPod and put it away. I spent the next day with my uncle, driving him to his doctor's appointment. Without me there, he'd have to have taken the DART and two buses. He had a spot on his lung, a strange shadow, his doctor wanted to biopsy. My intuition told me that he was too frail to survive the procedure, and the thought of him baking all morning in the Dallas heat, making his train and catching two connecting buses, to meet his death chilled me to the bone.

I dropped him off at the entrance of the VA and drove down the hill to park. I climbed back up the hill on foot, a steep hill he'd have to have huffed and puffed his way up from the bus stop otherwise. Inside, I asked the receptionist where I might find him. The lobby was busier than Grand Central Station at rush hour, and I moved through its multi-directional tumult until I finally found the examining room they'd placed him in.

He was already buttoning up his shirt.

"What happened?" I said.

"Oh, the doctor changed his mind," Ike told me. "He said the procedure was too dangerous, and he wasn't comfortable doing it."

I drove Ike back to his apartment. We spent the afternoon chatting over coffee at a bookstore. I had dinner with my sisters and I flew home the following day. I had every intention of listening to the second half of the lecture on my return flight, but things didn't work out that way.

On the flight in, I was in seat 16E, and my arrival gate, I noticed, was E16. This must have done something to my head, because on my return flight I sat in 18E, but as it turned out, I'd misread my ticket. The departure gate was

E18. My actual seat was an aisle seat almost at the back of the plane.

I settled in, put my iPod in my shirt pocket. From where I was sitting, I could see all the way up the aisle and I watched as a man, a late arrival, came dashing towards the back of the plane. He was sweating visibly, his blond hair matted brown in places it was so wet. The tails of his half-untucked Hawaiian shirt and his mustache were flying. He was clutching a briefcase and what looked like an enormous leather-bound Bible to his chest.

Perhaps it was his Bible—I tend to attract on-the-edge types—but somehow I knew this guy was not only heading for the empty seat next to mine but that he would invariably want to speak with me. Both of these things turned out to be true. He was, in fact, heading to the middle seat in my row. Standing over me, he juggled his Bible and his briefcase and checked his ticket, moist in his hand, against the seat numbers.

"I'm here," he said. "In the middle."

I unbuckled my seat belt and got up to let him in. He took a not small amount of time settling in, letting his sweat dry and placing his Bible and his briefcase on his pull-down tray. As the plane took off, I kept my eyes in front of me, hoping that this and my iBuds would serve as a DO NOT TRESPASS sign. Keeping his briefcase and his Bible on his lap, he nervously bounced his knees. He was wearing olive-drab shorts, and his legs were covered with little coils of coppery hair. When we reached altitude, I turned on my iPod and dialed up the second half of Tirzeh's lecture. In my peripheral vision, I watched as the guy tried to engage the woman in the window seat in conversation, but she was having none of it.

I closed my eyes and pushed my chair back, but it wasn't long before I thought I heard him speaking to me. I ignored it, but when he addressed me again, I caved. There was something too heartbreaking about this guy trying to speak to his seatmates and being completely ignored.

I took off my iBuds.

"Did you say something?" I asked him.

"I just thought I'd say hello," he said, "and perhaps speak to you for a moment about God."

"Ah, yes," I said, straightening up in my seat. "I thought that's what this would be about. What exactly about God would you like to know?"

"Oh, are you a religious man?" he said, brightening.

"Well, that's a complicated question."

"You're telling me," he said, shaking his head.

I don't remember exactly how the conversation meandered there, but eventually we got to his life story. He'd been raised a Catholic, he told me, but he had long ago turned his back on the church. His entire life, he'd had no use for religion, really, and so this whole thing was new to him. He'd never even read the Bible before. He hadn't quite made his way through it yet, but he felt he had to go around and spread the word of God. He knew he wasn't very good at it, but still . . .

"Maybe I should start at the beginning?" he said.

"Sure. Why not?" I said.

He owned a lighting design company in Florida, he told me. They were the people who'd install lights in your trees, you know, so that you could swim or barbecue at night. Everything was going well, too. He had more work than he could handle. He had had to hire a few extra people, and one of them was his son. Now, the thing of it is: he'd never been close to his children, but now that his son was working for him the two of them were getting closer and closer. He really enjoyed having his boy near him. It felt as though they were making up for lost time.

One day, though, he gets a call: *You'd better get here*, they tell him. *Your son has fallen out of a tree.*

"He'd been hanging lights high up in a palm tree and he lost his balance and fell."

No one told him how his son was. He had no idea if he was even alive.

"I had no experience, really, praying," he said, but as he dashed over to the project site he found himself saying, "Dear Lord, you can have my house, you can have my business, you can have my wife, if you'll just let my son live."

Uh-oh, I thought. *Not good. Not good at all.* I knew enough about theology to know that despite prominent counter examples in both the Bible and the Talmud, one is discouraged from placing limiting conditions on the Lord Almighty. The Holy One is famously arbitrary and willful. He cannot be subjected to our little deals and schemes. My seatmate's throwing of his wife into the pot made me cringe even more. How could he lump his wife into the same category as his business and his house?

When he arrived at the work site, he found his son alive, though barely. The boy had broken a dozen bones and ruptured a scad of internal organs, but they rushed him in an ambulance to the hospital and he survived.

Meanwhile, it wasn't long before the guy's business dried up. "Completely. I mean, we went from feast to famine in two short weeks. There was literally *no* work." As a consequence, he was unable to pay his mortgage and he lost his house. His wife had been flying to Phoenix on a regular basis to visit her daughter—she'd been married once before—and while she was out west she'd begun sleeping with her daughter's father-in-law. Now his marriage was over.

God had taken him at his word, he said, looking at me with a frank look on his face. I looked at him. We were silent for a moment.

"This may strike you as odd," I told him, "although perhaps it won't, but I happen to be listening to a lecture right now on the annulment of vows."

"That is surprising," he said.

"Yeah."

"Wow," he said softly, and even more softly, "Wow."

"It explains how to annul your vows."

"That's an extraordinary coincidence, don't you think?"

"Yeah. I mean, I've had these CDs for years. I never really listened to them until now, and now, for some reason, this is the one I thought to put on my iPod."

"As though it were a message meant for me."

"That's what I was thinking," I said.

"Wow."

He was silent again for a moment.

"But it's too late now, isn't it? I mean, everything's already gone," he said.

"I know, but at least from a Jewish perspective—I don't know how Christianity deals with these things—but perhaps you made this vow too quickly, under a kind of emotional duress, and could be released from it and get everything back."

He bit his upper lip. His knees bounced nervously under his pull-out tray.

I have to say: there was something endearing about this fellow, something endearing in the way he couldn't quite master the rudiments of evangelicalism. He had no slick presentation, no working overview of the Bible, no real understanding of theology. On the contrary, he was a shambolic mess, all flying shirttails and perspiration. Certainly he was the last person the woman in the window seat wanted to be stuck with for a two-hour flight, and who could blame her? Who would ever listen to a man like that about matters of life and death?

Still, my heart went out to him. I wanted to help him out of his predicament. I mean, what were the chances that he'd tell his story to a stranger who was listening to a lecture about how to annul your vows?

As it turned out, though, he had no interest in the rabbinic opt-out clause I was offering him.

"I don't care if I end up living under a bridge," he said. "I can put my arms around my son, and that's all that matters to me."

As far as he was concerned, he'd had a profound experience. He'd felt the hand of God in his life, and it wasn't an overly gentle hand either. Taking him at his word, God had thrown him into bankruptcy, into home forfeiture, into cuckoldry, but he had his son, and it would be churlish to complain.

"Everything has its cost," he told me.

Something in the way he said this made me think of my uncle.

"But even in the book of Job," I told him, "God knocks Job around a bit, but in the end, Job not only gets new children to replace the ones he lost, but God restores his possessions *and* his health."

"Does he?"

"Yeah."

"Yeah," he said, nodding towards his Bible, "I haven't really gotten that far yet."

I offered to burn a copy of the CD for him, in case he changed his mind. He gave me his address, and when I arrived home I made the disc and dropped it in the mail.

Not long after that, I received a letter from him. He'd listened to the lecture, he wrote, and he was grateful for the gift of it, but he was adamant. He'd made his agreement with God. He was content with the terms of the deal and had no interest in annulling his vow.

I leaned back in my chair and tossed his letter onto a pile of papers on my desk. Through the windows of my study, I watched the postman in his little truck making his halting dash from mailbox to mailbox on the other side of the street. I picked up the phone to call Ike. I was still worrying about him, though I suppose the guy on the plane was right: everything has its cost, and there's only so much you can do putting yourself between a man and the bargain that he's made.

PRE-SWEETENED
WITHOUT SUGAR

We set about our work with the alacrity of little advertising men. On our hands and knees on the linoleum floor, the crayons from our big thirty-two Crayola pack scattered between us, we devoted a Sunday morning to the task.

My sisters were behind the whole thing. They'd seen the ad in the funny papers—they could read; I couldn't—or maybe our mother had pointed it out to them.

Funny Face packaged soft drink mixes were new on the market back in 1964. They were meant to compete with

Kool-Aid, the original granulated drink mix. Crammed full of cyclamates, they were advertised as "pre-sweetened without sugar."

Each flavor had a different Funny Face character on the package, each drawn, snaggle-toothed and cockle-eyed, as though by the imprecise hand of a child. Injun Orange was an orange in war paint and feathers. Chinese Cherry was a slant-eyed cherry with a Hop Sing pigtail. Lefty Lemon was a baseball-pitching lemon. Loud-Mouth Lime had a big mouth. Rootin'-Tootin' Raspberry was a cowboy, and the front man of the bunch was a beach bum named Goofy Grape.

The company was running a coloring contest. Kids were asked to color a picture of Goofy Grape and send it in. First prize was a Funny Face soft drink stand that you could set up in your own front yard. Second place was a wristwatch with a picture of Goofy Grape on the crystal, third place was twenty-five dollars worth of coupons or something like that.

I was a better colorer than my sisters, and my picture came out best, and as my sisters were filling out the entry form on my behalf—name, age, address—a thought occurred to them: as impressive as my picture was, wouldn't it be even more impressive if it had been colored not by a five-year-old but by a three-year-old kid, and what harm would there be, really, if they knocked a couple of years off my age and filled it in as three?

In a moment of childish paranoia—we were Jewish children, after all—they had second thoughts. What would happen if the judges checked and discovered that I was really five?

Two little Macbeths, in so far there was no turning back, they decided instead of changing my age back to five to fill in our brother Ethan's name on the entry form, since he was really three.

When, a few weeks later, a small purple package arrived, I knew instantly what it was.

"I won! I won!" I shouted to Annie Quattlebaum in the front hall as she brought in the mail. Annie had worked for my grandmother years before, helping to raise my father and his brothers, and now, fallen on hard times, she was living with us. "I've won the Goofy Grape watch!"

"Oh, no, dear," Annie said, holding the package back from me. "This is for Ethan. You see, it's got his name on the address label."

Now, the curious thing is, I don't remember what happened next. No one, including me, actually remembers what happened between the arrival of the package in its purple wrapping and Ethan's taking possession of the watch. I can only imagine I protested, first to Annie, then to my parents, but that somehow, in the intervening weeks, my sisters had forgotten all about their clever subterfuge. My parents, as gullible as the judges it seems, never wondered how their three-year-old might have colored well enough to win a national competition, or perhaps they simply couldn't be interested in our childish quarrels. Maybe Annie put her foot down and forbade me to even speak of it to them. It's reasonable, I suppose. On the face of it, my claims—that I'd colored the picture but that believing the judges would find the work of a three-year-old more compelling, my sisters had changed the age and then, covering their tracks, inserted Ethan's name in a contest he just happened to win—seem exactly the sort of thing a lying child might come up with.

Whatever the case, Ethan was given the watch. When he was twelve or so, having no personal stake in it, he scratched Goofy Grape's face off the crystal and tossed it into the back of a bathroom cupboard.

Over the years, the story became one of those anecdotes that are shared in families, a sweet little story about two bossy little girls running their little brother's life. The story, in its many retellings, always skips the part between the arrival of the purple package and Ethan's being given the watch, and all these years later, I find that's the only part of the story that interests me.

WOODEN NICKELS

Tiger was the first man I ever saw with a beard. I was only five or six years old. We were living in Amarillo then, and Tiger, passing through on his way to Vegas, stopped at our house for the seder. He was married at the time, his wife a heavy-set gentile woman with a short blonde ponytail, whose career as a dancer he managed.

"She was a very intelligent girl," my father told me years later. "Her father was a college professor, I think."

The Tigers—Mr. and Mrs.—roared into our driveway in the painted-over hearse they traveled and lived in—

sometimes, I was told, but not anymore, with a pet monkey. They bounded inside like the tigers prancing around in human clothing in *The Story of Little Black Sambo*, a book I loved, Tiger presenting each of the children with a small wooden coin that had a caricature of his face—grinning, leering, winking—stamped onto it encircled by a logo that read:

DON'T TAKE ANY WOODEN NICKELS

Tiger was my father's cousin. They were born eight days apart, and they grew up as close as brothers, if not twins. First sons of sisters, they played together, performed magic tricks together. They were bar mitzvahed together, and they were always being compared, with Tiger always coming up short.

"Why can't Jack be more like Irvin?" his mother, Rose, wrote to her sister Mimi when—incredulously I checked the date on the letter—the boys were not yet two.

Except for Tiger's echt-beatnik affectations—the savage van Dyke, the mustache curled up at the ends, the hipster's lope and drawl—they even resembled each other. They had the same tall forehead, the same wiry dark hair, the same posture, the same broad shoulders, the same slender legs;

their skin was the same olive color; they were the same height.

At the seder table, I felt as though I were looking at two versions of the same man, one civilized, the other feral, and this was confusing to me. Dad was the picture of sober rectitude. A young father of four, returning from work each day promptly at six in his dark suit and his narrow tie, he was like a Lutheran pastor in a Bergman film: strict, exacting, a disciplinarian. It was unfathomable to me that he could so warmly welcome into our home his wild and untamed twin.

FORTY OR SO years later, my uncle Richard sits down next to me on the couch, and gives me a penetrating look. Richard is my father's youngest brother. With his ochre skin and shock of white hair, he looks like a Cuban aristocrat.

"Nephew," he says. He often calls me Nephew. I call him Favorite Uncle. It's a nickname he gave himself. "What're the chances do you think I could talk your brother into looking into all of Tiger's stuff for me?"

"Well, it's hard to say," I tell him. "I mean, it's hard to get Ethan to do something he doesn't want to do."

I say this with a slight edge in my voice, as though it were a defect in my brother's character, but then I think: *What's so wrong with not doing things you don't want to do?*

Tiger had been dead for a year or so.

"And he had all his stuff stored in a barn on a chicken farm in upstate New York," Richard tells me, "not far from where Ethan lives. Couldn't be more than, I don't know, thirty miles from his house. No one knows if any of it's worth anything, but I'm paying a hundred dollars a month to this farmer up there to keep all that crap. Not me personally, but the estate. I'm the executor. None of Jack's nieces or his nephew want any of it, but if there's something of value there . . ."

"Like what?" I say.

"Oh, hell, I don't know. Jack was supposed to have collected posters . . ."

"Posters?"

". . . circus posters, vintage circus posters, and I don't know if they're worth anything, but if they are, we might as well do something with them, don't you think?"

"Well, I guess . . ."

"So if Ethan won't do it . . ."

"He won't."

". . . if the estate paid your way, would you be willing to go up there and take a look at it all for me?"

TIGER HAD ACTUALLY mentioned this stuff to me, or at least a part of it a few years before. We were heading out to a farm in Giddings one Sunday morning to buy Samantha a dog. Barbara and Sami were already in the car when the phone rang. I picked it up, and the voice on the other end roared out a kind of hipster growl: *"S'Tiiiiggggerrr!"*

I'd never gotten a call from Tiger before, but I'd been told about these calls by my sister Susan who used to get them frequently. Tiger faxed her something once, and behind the document he'd intended to send—placed crookedly on the machine's screen, I guess—was a copy of his résumé. After every listing, Susan told me, there was a line explaining why each project had failed: "investors backed out" . . . "lost funding" . . . "idea stolen."

"Tiger, is that you?" I said.

It was, he said, and he was calling because he had a collection of books, collected over a lifetime, that he didn't know what to do with.

"I was talking to your dad, and he told me that you liked books, and so I thought you might want to have them."

This was an odd way of putting it, I thought. It wasn't really a question of liking or disliking books, although I suppose there are people who dislike books. Certainly over the years I've met a few, especially in Texas, where often they serve on school boards. Rather, it was a question of whether the books themselves were worth reading.

They were stored at a friend's place in upstate New York, he told me, and all I had to do was rent a U-Haul—"But it's gonna take a U-Haul"—and I could have as many as I wanted. "I mean, some of them are real classics."

Because my life was fairly unsettled at the time—we were living in Austin again, with no clear plans of staying or leaving; I had no idea where I might keep a U-Haulful of books—and also because Tiger's reputation preceded him, I declined.

But now, with Richard explaining to me that half of Tiger's worldly possessions were stored in a barn on a chicken farm in upstate New York—the other half was in a storage locker in Dallas—and with the estate offering to foot the bill, the absurdity of the thing appealed to me.

And I told him I'd be happy to do it whether Ethan joined me or not.

WHEN I WAS a kid, Tiger's occasional visits to Lubbock sent a kind of terror through the family. No one wanted him there, but no one knew how to ask him to leave. He'd arrive with an empty suitcase, and by the time he departed, it would be full of my grandfather's old clothes. My parents took him to dinner at places they never went to or didn't care if they ever returned to. "Do you have apple pandowdy?" he asked their waitress once when she came for the dessert order. "Makes your eyes light up and your stomach say howdy?" He filled the pockets of what had been until that afternoon my grandfather's sports coat with dozens of unpeeled shrimp from the all-you-can-eat buffet. "A little something for later," he said, patting the fabric of the coat, and he loved nothing better than to lie on the couch where he slept, eating sardines out of the can, dipping pieces of rye bread into the oil.

"This is the great Jack Tiger, famous movie producer from New York City!" we'd overhear him making cold calls in my sisters' bedroom.

During one of his visits, Ethan, feeling unwell, slipped out of the living room and went into our parents' bedroom to watch television.

"Did he make you sick?" our grandmother asked him, coming into the room and finding him there. "He makes me sick, too!"

Tiger always seemed to be traveling through Texas during a family crisis. Though he'd known nothing of her illness or her death, he showed up, quite out of the blue, at my mother's funeral, wailing inconsolably—more inconsolably than the actual mourners who were pretty inconsolable—and needing a place to stay.

"Tonight: all right, Jack," his aunt Jeanette said as she made our sofa up as a bed for him, "but after that, you've got to get out of here. You've got to let these good people alone."

At my mother's shivah, he boxed me into a corner to talk screenwriting. "A close-up is punctuation, punctuation!" he growled at me. "You go in close on a tube of red lipstick. Why? Punctuation! That's all it is!"

At sunrise the following morning, I rode with my father, as he drove Tiger to the bus terminal. The two of them sat up front—they were only fifty-eight at the time—and from the backseat they looked like they always did, like two versions of the same person, Dad the well-dressed, well-kempt version, all colored in between the lines, and Tiger a whirl of frenetic energy, his stuffing coming out of his seams as he rambled on obsessively about secondary Japanese markets and direct-to-home video.

As I listened to their conversation, lines from William Blake's *Songs of Innocence and Experience* kept going through my head:

> *Tyger Tyger, burning bright,*
> *In the forests of the night:*
> *What immortal hand or eye,*
> *Could frame thy fearful symmetry?*

I CALL DAVE Cole, the chicken farmer in upstate New York, to let him know that my brother and I are considering coming up and taking a look at Tiger's things.

"I'm dividing the film from the rest," he tells me. "It's an immense amount of material. A lot of it is 3-D. Very futuristic. I have to take my lady friend to the hospital today to visit her niece, but once we're back it shouldn't take me more'n two hours to go through the rest of it. But you're gonna need more'n a car just to haul the films away."

"Do you really want a *carload* of film?" Ethan says when I call him afterward. Though he's willing to accompany me, he reiterates that he's not really interested in doing any of this. Disenthused by his reaction, I put off calling Dave

Cole again, but then Dave calls me. He's found forty copies of a 3-D *Frankenstein*. "It's heartbreaking to throw all this stuff out. There're twenty-five milk cartons, all crammed with books!"

He asks me where I live, and when I tell him, he tells me he has a son-in-law in Atlanta who just had a stroke. "Forty-one years old, he can stand on his left foot, but he dudn't even know his right foot is there. He was twenty-five years in the army, lied about his age to get in. No, he must be forty-seven now."

"Forty-seven's still young," I say.

"Still young, yes, it is," Dave says. "Dr. Richard tells me you're coming up here to check everything out."

Dave calls Richard, an orthodontist, "Dr. Richard."

I tell him I'll talk to Dr. Richard and to my brother Ethan and see what we can do.

"You were never out here. It's sixty feet long and maybe fifty feet deep. We left a path so you could move through it to get at everything, but then it became too much and we had to fill in all the paths."

MAYBE IT WAS his beard when I was a kid, but Tiger always seemed two-thirds animal to me, as though he were a real tiger forced, for some reason (*Why can't you be more like Irvin?*), to live in the world as a man. He could never find a place for himself within human society. His appetites were too large, his touch too fierce, his dreams burned too brightly in the furnace of his brain.

At sixteen, he changed his name from Jack Goldman to J. G. Tiger.

"The *G* was for Goldman," Dad told me. "And *Tiger* was because if you meet somebody named Tiger, you're not going to forget it."

He dropped out of East Texas State Teachers College after half a semester and ran away with the circus. In Canada, he left the circus to become a tout at the track. He returned to Dallas with a fat roll of cash, driving a 1952 Lincoln hardtop named El Tigre. Among El Tigre's custom features was a hood ornament shaped like a leaping tiger. Tiger drove El Tigre in the Dallas heat with the windows up and a telephone handset pressed against his ear, so he appeared to be conducting business on a car phone in air-conditioned comfort.

He opened up a recording studio, though he never made a record. For a while, he had an opium dope show. He promoted restaurants and wrestling matches. He even wrestled himself, unspectacularly by all accounts, as the Baby Tiger.

Eventually, he joined the marines. Stationed at El Toro in California, he served his country as the night water tender on a military golf course, turning the sprinklers off by the dawn's early light and on again at the twilight's last gleaming.

After the military, Tiger invented Birdicure.

"Parakeets were very popular as pets in the fifties, but they'd get sick and die," Dad told me, "and so Tiger set up a

laboratory in Aunt Rose's house. He figured out the appropriate dosage of penicillin for a bird, and he put that amount
into tablet form."

He hired children from the neighborhood. They sat at
Aunt Rose's kitchen table, stuffing the pills into the bottles
and Scotch-taping the instructions to them with their little
hands.

Dad was an officer in the navy, stationed at the time in
Hawaii.

"There was no air conditioning, so your mother and I
slept with our windows, these big lanai windows, open."

One night, Dad couldn't sleep. It was two in the morning,
and he was lying in bed. Everything was quiet, and through
the open window, he could hear a little thudding sound far
off in the distance. *Pop-pop-pop-pop-pop.* He couldn't stop
listening to it. It kept getting louder and louder until eventually he recognized the sound: it was a motorcycle. The
sound kept getting louder as the motorcycle got closer, and
nearly half an hour later, he heard it *putt-putt-putt*ing onto
the base, then onto their street, then into their cul-de-sac,
where it stopped. Dead silence. A moment later, there's a
knock on their door.

Dad gets out of bed. He puts on his robe. He answers the
door. A special airmail deliveryman in leathers and goggles
hands him a letter.

Dad looks at the return address. It's from Birdicure, Inc.,
Dallas, Texas.

It's from Tiger, of course. He wants Dad to tear out the yellow pages from the phone book listing all the pet stores on the island and send them back to him by return post, in an envelope he's provided. The special deliveryman waits while Dad does all this. Taking the envelope, he fires up his bike. Dad climbs back into bed, and for the next half hour he's up, listening to the engine getting softer and softer as the motorcycle gets farther and farther away.

"But Birdicure was a success," Dad tells me. "Tiger went to New York and got Birdicure listed with Kress and Woolworth, and he actually made some money on it."

And with that money, Tiger finally did what he always wanted to do, which was to make movies, of course.

TIGER MADE ONLY two films that I know of.

The first, from 1957, was called *Rock Baby Rock It*. Billed as "the original rockabilly rhythm 'n' blues cult classic filmed on location in Dallas," it featured local bands from the period. The plot: "Every bobcat, kool kitten and crazy combo in town get together to save the local Hot Rock club and give the mob the 'weenie' once and for all."

Tiger's second film came out three years later. *Many Ways to Sin* is the story of a magician named Dante. Lately, he's been having trouble distinguishing between reality and the world of his stage illusions (a problem Tiger was no doubt familiar with). Someone has been murdering Dante's beautiful assistants—Velma, who assists in his guillotine act, for instance, is found decapitated—and the film plays out as a cat-and-mouse between Inspector Evans, who is investigating the murders, and Dante, who may or may not be committing them.

A friend of mine recently found a black-and-white glossy from the film online. In it, the actor playing Dante levitates one of his leggy assistants while two other assistants, equally leggy, look on. The whole thing seems fairly amateurish. Dante's beard, which resembles Tiger's, is clearly and clumsily glued on.

Though the film, retitled *Victimes du Démon*, played in Paris at the Midi-Minuit for a week in 1966 and was released as *Immer bei Nacht* in Germany the same year, no print of it survives.

Dad saw it. "Tiger had a private showing in New York. It was sad, really. He'd write these movies, do all the production work and the rewrites, but it was a shell game. He'd talk all these star-struck kids into acting for free, then he'd con people into investing in it. But then he'd run out of money, because he was living on the investors' money, plus he had expenses with all the equipment and everything, so he'd write a new movie, and he'd sell the idea for *that* movie to *new* investors, and he'd take the money from the second movie to start making the first one, and so on and so on. His problem was he never wanted to make a hundred dollars, he only wanted to make a million."

• • •

THOUGH NONE OF Tiger's other film projects ever saw the light of day—*idea stolen . . . funding lost . . . investors backed out*—he spent the last years of his life laying the groundwork for what promised to be the biggest deal he'd ever pull off. Everything was in place. All he needed was a Letter of Intent from the Indians. He wasn't well, that was the only thing, and he worried that he might not live long enough to ink in the contracts, and so he asked Dad to come with him to Tahlequah, hoping his presence there might reassure the Cherokee.

Dad flew to Tulsa. He rented a car and picked Tiger up at the Greyhound terminal. But it was a wasted trip, he told me. "Tiger's cancer was in remission. Supposedly. But the chemo had taken its toll, and he looked a mess. He had a coat and a tie, but he was wearing yellow cotton pants with bright yellow suspenders designed to look like yardsticks. His hair was sparse, and what little he had left was dyed a vibrant red. His beard and his mustache were also a bright red. He was wearing a kangaroo cap. And—oh, yeah—a black cape. His shoes were two-toned golf shoes with tassels handed down to him years ago from your grandfather. He'd unscrewed the cleats so he could walk on them. But when he crossed his legs, you could see the little holes on their bottoms, and he was so weak he could barely walk, even with a couple of canes."

Still, he was well versed in what was going on with the Indians in New York State. "They were the first to put in a

casino, and they'd made a fortune with it, and Tiger was trying to duplicate that with the Cherokee."

There was only one sticking point. "No one was going to
put up a dime until the Indians gave up their sovereignty.
They couldn't be held accountable in an American court
otherwise." The investors wanted a level playing field, and
it was Tiger's job to convince the Indians to sign a Letter of
Intent, legally renouncing their sovereignty. And it wasn't
only the Cherokee. Tiger had been speaking to Indian chiefs
throughout the Plains states and the Southwest, riding from
reservation to reservation on a thirty-day bus pass. Things
were moving forward on all fronts, but the Cherokee, Tiger
felt, were ready to sign. He'd found a resort in Pennsylvania—
because the Cherokee had once been in Pennsylvania, they
qualified to buy land and go into business there—but it
wasn't only going to be casinos.

"Oh, he had a lot of ideas," Dad says. Mostly, he wanted
to make movies at the resort. "That way, working on Indian
land, you wouldn't have to pay union scale, you see?"

"And what are you saying to him as he's telling you all
these things?" I ask my father.

"I'm just listening. I'm trying to get him to scale everything back. First do one thing, then worry about the next,
but there's no arguing with him. I mean, to tell the Indians
about museums and the movies, you're just going to over-
whelm them. Let's see if we can first get the gambling and
then worry about the other ramifications."

"And when he spoke to the chief, did he do that or did he mention everything?"

"No, he mentioned everything."

I try to imagine Tiger, pacing in his decleated golf shoes and his black cape, waxing euphoric over the river of money that will flow to the Cherokee from the casinos he will build and the films he will make on their ancestral lands once, thanks to certain loopholes in the American tax code, they renounce their sovereignty.

"You have to understand," Dad says. "The chief is the chief, but he's also just a working guy, probably in his mid- to late fifties. He's polite, he's considerate, but he's not going to sign any Letter of Intent. He's not giving away his people's sovereignty. Jack invites him to lunch, but the chief's got other meetings, so we take some of the office people out, so Jack can talk over the deal. This all takes about two hours, and then we're back in Tulsa. Tiger gets on the bus—he's got his thirty-day pass—and he's off to talk to another tribe. And that was Tahlequah."

A WEEK ON my calendar finally opens up, and I call Dave Cole and arrange to come out to his farm. We agree on a date and a time, and he gives me overly precise road directions which include the location of various speed traps and a lengthy history of his brother's alcoholism. Ethan meets me at the airport, and the next morning, we head out. Ethan and I have been studying Yiddish and Hebrew together twice a week on the phone and we've become closer perhaps than we've ever been as adults. Two variations on the same genetic theme, we share a lifetime of references—familial, cultural, personal—and are sensitive to the subtlest change in each other's intonation. Instantly responsive to the smallest suggestion, we can turn on a dime, leaping from reference to reference, following each other into an imaginary world.

Somehow, over the course of our studies, we'd invented an entire classroom led by a strict teacher named Mrs. Pilsner. The good student was named Jimmy, and the bad student—at the time, I had no reason to think it had anything to do with Tiger—was called Jack.

One afternoon, Ethan was quizzing me on verb tenses, and I either didn't know the answer or I hesitated in giving it. His voice, over the telephone, grew instantly stern. "Don't tell me you didn't study!" he said.

As instantly, I assumed the quaking voice of a miserable, humiliated child.

"I'm sorry, Mrs. Pilsner. I didn't have time to study because . . ."

Ethan became Mrs. Pilsner: "No more of your excuses, Jack!"

"Yes, Mrs. Pilsner. But it's just that my father . . ."

"I said enough of your excuses!"

". . . was drunk and raving in the kitchen. He hit my mother and sent her to the hospital and . . ."

"Does *anybody* here know the correct answer?"

"I do, Mrs. Pilsner!" I called out in the voice of another student.

Mrs. Pilsner's voice sweetens. She's clearly talking now to the teacher's pet.

"Ah, Jimmy, yes! Go on. Please, share the correct answer with everyone." Her voice grows cross again: "Are you listening, Jack?"

Jack, downcast, says, "Yes, Mrs. Pilsner."

"You had better be!"

The scenario was fluid. Sometimes I played Mrs. Pilsner and Ethan played Jimmy or Jack, and there were other students as well: Sally, an inattentive flirt in love with Biff, a jock who, though *he* never studied and never knew the correct answer, was never shamed by Mrs. Pilsner, a circumstance that only increased Jack's sense of humiliation. Jack's life and his love of learning were being destroyed by Mrs. Pilsner, but Ethan and I were having a great time.

ETHAN ACTUALLY WORKED for Tiger, though only for a week or so. Tiger was shooting a film in New York called *The Perils of P.K.*, and Dad had gotten Ethan the job in the hopes of advancing his acting career.

"Move all this mail from here," Tiger told Ethan, pointing to one side of his office, "to here," he said, pointing to another. "And if anybody calls for a Joe Green, he's not in. Joe

Green is not in, and David Davidian is also not in. You got that? There is no Joe Green here and no David Davidian."

"Can I quit?" Ethan asked our mother before his second week was through.

"I used to see him on the streets of New York," Ethan tells me in the car, "and there was always a moment of shock, because he not only looked homeless but he looked so much like Dad, and for a moment, I'd think it *was* Dad, sitting on the curb or on a fire hydrant with his pants rolled up to his knees."

ETHAN AND I turn in at a sign that says COOPERTON FARM FRESH EGGS and arrive at a house with black shutters and yellow siding. I walk to the front porch and knock on the door. Ethan gets out of the car. He puts his hands into his back and leans into them, stretching.

"Are you getting a kind of *Deliverance* feeling here?" he says, looking around the place.

No one answers the door, and I call Dave on my cell phone. A telephone starts ringing inside his house. When I hang up, the phone inside the house stops ringing.

I call Richard and tell him that we've arrived, but that no one seems to be here.

He tells me not to worry, that he'll call Dave, and a moment later, the phone starts ringing inside the house again. After it stops, Richard calls me back.

"Nobody answered," he says.

"I know," I say. "We can hear the phone ringing inside the house."

"Well, give him a minute. He'll be there."

I can't shake the feeling that someone's inside the house, watching us. I look around the property. There's a rusted-out pickup truck with flat tires. Branches from the bushes are growing through its broken windows. The earth seems to be rising up around it, reclaiming it, along with a long metal chicken coop that's lying on the ground, twisted up like a broken accordion.

I get my camera out, but there's only one exposure left. I search through my bag, but I'm out of film.

We passed a little store about a mile back, and I suggest to Ethan that as long as Dave isn't here, we could dash back and pick up some film.

"And maybe he'll come back in the meantime."

When we return to the farm, there's a piece of white paper hanging on the front door of the house.

"Hey, that wasn't here before?"

We get out of the car. The note on the door reads:

KEPT LATE AT COUNTY FAIR IMPOSSIBLE

TO GET BACK SEE MY DAUGHTER

HOUSE END OF ROAD.

DAVE

We look at each other. I knock on the door, but no one answers. I dial Dave's number. The phone in the house starts ringing. I want to shout, *I know you're in there!* But I don't, of course. None of this makes sense. The time sequences make no sense. If Dave were being kept late at the fair, when did he put this note on the door? *Before* going to the fair that he couldn't get away from now?

"Which end of the road do you think he even means?" I say.

Ethan looks at me, as though to say, *You see, this is exactly why I don't do these sorts of things.*

WE DRIVE TO the main road. I ring the doorbell at a couple of houses, but no one answers here either. We return to the farm and walk around the property on our own, but we can't find anything resembling a barn filled with canisters of film. It's already midafternoon. I'm ready, though reluctantly, to call it a day, and Ethan's heart was never in it to begin with. As we're heading back, we pass a large two-story house with a big circular drive. It's right where the road bends, and it occurs to me that a person might think of this bend as a kind of end.

"Do you think that's Dave Cole's daughter's house?" I say.

"I doubt it," Ethan says, slowing to a stop.

"Listen," I say. "There's music coming from the back. If someone's there, maybe they can at least tell us how to find the daughter."

Sighing, Ethan puts the car into Park.

"Hello?" I call, walking towards the back. "Hello?" No one

answers my call. The moment I return to our car, though, someone pulls out from behind the house. Already speeding, tires squealing, throwing gravel up from the driveway, the driver tears out onto the main road.

I jump into the passenger seat. "Follow that car!" I shout at Ethan.

"What?" he says, looking confused.

"Follow that car!"

"No! I will not! Follow that car!"

"Why *not*? Come on! They're getting away!"

As though I were Laurel and he Hardy, Ethan gives me a slow-burn that says, *Do I really have to explain this to you?*

"Well, when you put it that way," I say.

We sit in the car for a moment. A teenager, with thick glasses and thicker acne, trots past us on a horse. He leans down, peering into the car. I lean across Ethan to shout up at him. "Hey, do you by any chance know where we might find Dave Cole's daughter's house?"

He stares at us coldly as he passes by.

"Great!" I say to Ethan. "First Blake and now Yeats!"

"What are you *talking* about!" Ethan says.

He shifts into Drive and is about to pull out onto the road when a car swims up next to ours, blocking us in. The driver, a woman, sits face-to-face with Ethan. She introduces herself as Dave Cole's daughter, and she invites us to follow her back to the farm. Once we're there, she leads us straight to the barn. It's right behind the house down a well-marked path. I don't know how we could have missed it.

Inside, everything is pretty much as Dave described it on the phone: a mountain of stuff, Tiger's things, sixty feet long, fifty feet wide, maybe ten feet high.

Dave's daughter tells us that she and Jack were friends. He had all this stuff in a storage locker in Manhattan, but when the locker began to flood her father offered him the use of his barn. It took fourteen trips back and forth between Middletown and Manhattan to haul it all up.

"Well, I'll leave you to it," she says.

Ethan and I nose around a bit. I open one of the boxes of books and take out a cheap paperback. Inside the front cover is written "Movie of the Week?" There are boxes that look like someone simply swiped his arm across a messy desk, throwing everything into it, intending to sort through it all later. We find a bag of coins and a couple of thirty-year-old girlie magazines and cards for an escort service. There are large canisters of 16-mm films and hand-drawn posters for a never-released comedy called "Out to Lunch."

The barn isn't airtight. The wooden walls have openings in them. A few of the windows are broken. Through them, I can see that the sun has already set. The sky is a dark red, charred with blue. We've only been in the barn about thirty minutes, but it's already too dark to see, and the amount of stuff is overwhelming. Ethan and I barely get through a fraction of it.

Back home, I call Dave Cole and ask him to send me a few canisters of the film. Richard pays him to cart everything else to the dump. I store the film in my office at work, thinking one day I'll hire a projectionist to screen it, but of course I never do. Years later, I'm out of the country when I see an email on the college list-serv: torrential rains have flooded the top floor of my building. The only damage seemed to have been sustained by canisters of film stored there. It takes me a moment, so far from home, to realize that the office in question is my office and that the films are Jack's.

NEAR THE END of his life, Tiger disappeared, and no one knew where he was for days until he phoned Richard from Harrisburg, needing cash. Richard called Dad. Dad called the Harrisburg police. The Harrisburg police found Tiger sleeping in the park. They committed him to a psychiatric hospital for observation. They said they'd release him to a family member, so Dad flew up. The cancer had returned and was affecting Tiger's brain. Tiger believed the VA had a hit list of patients they'd been treating too long. He was on the list, but he'd fled before they could zap him with their lasers.

All he had on him when Dad arrived at the hospital was a paper sack filled with contracts and letters of intent for the Indians. The Plains tribes were having a big powwow, and Tiger was hoping to get back to Oklahoma where he could find all the chiefs in one place. Dad brought him to Dallas. Working in concert, his cousins placed him in a Jewish home for the elderly. Tiger told the staff that he was adopted, that he wasn't really Jewish, and that he had no right being there. As a result, they put him on a locked Alzheimer's ward. Richard saw to the paperwork, trying to get him his military benefits, but he couldn't get too far. Even when he was in the marines, Tiger had used his sister Marion's Social Security number.

Tiger grew listless and lethargic on the Alzheimer's ward. He told Dad he wished somebody from the family would take him out for the day. He wanted to see a television with this year's football games on it. The TVs in the retirement home showed games that were at least two years old.

I hate to think of him, dying there. I prefer to think of him sleeping in the park in Harrisburg, sprawled upon the ground beneath his tree, dressed, like the tigers in *Little Black Sambo*, in his dapper human clothing, his yellow pants and his yardstick suspenders, my grandfather's snazzy golf shoes with the cleats removed, an elegant, flowing cape like the cape he wore when he wrestled, magnificently, as the Baby Tiger, his extravagant mustaches and his beard dyed a vibrant red in the hopes of masking his tiger stripes, the fearful symmetry of his savage heart reconciled at last.

EVERYBODY'S LOT

I was meeting a colleague at a pizza place called Everybody's. I'd arrived early so I could go to the Chabad House beforehand. It was just down the street. The rabbi and I were studying the *Tanya* together, a mystical text about the righteous and the wicked and the rest of us in between.

I pulled into the parking lot behind the line of stores. I hadn't quite realized that Everybody's had its own parking lot on the other side of the building. There were signs in this parking lot listing all the businesses you could patronize while being parked here, and Everybody's wasn't one of them.

YOUR CAR WILL BE IMPOUNDED, blah blah blah, et cetera et cetera, the sign said, above the list of approved shops.

Now, I could have done a lot of things. I could have gotten back into my car and pulled into the lot on the other side. I could have walked through the back door of the Starbucks, dallied for a moment, taken off my coat, maybe even made a purchase, before walking out the front, confounding whoever might be observing me. I could have driven to the Chabad House and parked there for an hour and driven back.

Instead, I told myself that it's easy enough to put up signs like these, threatening this and threatening that, and quite another thing to employ a person to enforce your rules and carry out your threats.

I come from a long line of rule breakers. As a child, I was taught by the example of these elders that everything is negotiable. Nothing is written in stone. My grandfather Archie was essentially a draft dodger, sent to America in 1921 at the age of sixteen to avoid conscription into the Russian army. He and his sons after him made a fine art of walking freely through the world. My uncle Bernard was perhaps the most adept at this. Visiting friends at the hospital, Bernard parked in the Doctors Only spaces. Going into a restaurant to see how long the wait might be, he'd come out nibbling on things from the salad bar. He'd leave his own reception at a hotel and wander into other people's receptions. Moving through the receiving line, he'd introduce himself to the hosts, congratulate them on the occasion, and invite them to ours before helping himself to a little something from the buffet.

I wasn't like that as a child. I was a nervous kid, fretful, generally expecting the worst. The world was a dangerous place, and you never knew who might be watching you, following you, keeping track of you, perhaps even intending you harm.

Both of these impulses were alive in me as I stepped out of my car. On the one hand, I felt free to park in the wrong lot and to walk out to the street and away from the stores towards the Chabad House in broad daylight. On the other, I worried that someone *might* in fact be watching me. There was a man smoking a cigarette in the doorway of one of the businesses listed on the signs. I stared at him as I walked past. He gave me an impassive look in return.

But was he merely taking a break or was he, in fact, monitoring the lot?

I couldn't tell, and in the end, it was my paranoia that undid me. I was *feeling* paranoid, true, but because I have a tendency to *be* a little paranoid, I told myself I was *only* being paranoid, and dismissing healthy paranoia as its unhealthy twin, I walked down the street to the Chabad House where, for an hour, the rabbi and I made our imperfect progress through the hierarchies of the human soul.

Entering Everybody's an hour later, I'd forgotten all about the car.

I took a seat and waited for Kip to arrive.

Kip was the director of our program, and he and I were meeting to review the semester and evaluate the students and discuss the syllabi and perform the thousand and one other tedious tasks required of college professors. I'd taken a table near the door and was waiting for him when I noticed that the man sitting at the bar looked familiar.

Hey, isn't that that famous movie star? I said to myself. *No, no, I think it is!*

Though the movie star was famous and had been for years, for some reason, I couldn't remember his name. He'd been in everything. I'd seen him in dozens of films, going all the way back to the early 1980s, or maybe even the late '70s, but still I couldn't remember his name. I tried to get a better look at him, hoping to jog my memory, though to tell you the truth, I wasn't sure if it was really him or not.

I mean, I *thought* it was him, it looked like him, but I wasn't entirely sure.

I made a trip to the bathroom in order to come back to my table and get a look at him from a different angle, and from this other angle, the guy, whoever he was, didn't look like the movie star at all. No, he was just some guy hanging out at the bar, chatting with the bartender, but then the bartender took a photo of him with his phone, and I realized: *No, wait, it* is *that guy!*

Getting off his stool, the movie star turned around to head out. He walked past my table, and as he did, he ducked his head and stared through the windows at the lowering sky, zipping up his windbreaker, and there it was: the flattened nose, the full head of hair brushed back in a rakish pompadour, the steely blue-eyed gaze, all of which I'd seen countless times in countless movies, thirty feet tall, or whatever it is, on the silver screen.

He ducked out and was gone, and when Kip showed up a few minutes later, I said to him, "Man, you'll never guess who was in here just now?"

"Who?" Kip said, sliding down into the booth.

"I can't remember his name, but, you know, he's that really big movie star."

Kip squinted. "Who's this, you're saying?"

"You know him. I mean, *everybody* knows him. He's really famous. But for some reason—I don't know why—his name has left my head. But you've seen him in a million things. I mean, he's been in, like, everything."

"Yeah? Like what?"

"Oh, I mean, he's been in a million things, but I can't . . . for some reason . . . the only thing that comes to mind is . . . well, he was in . . . I mean, this was years ago, but he was in a movie called *The Falcon and the Snowman.*"

Kip shook his head. "Yeah, I never saw it."

"You know, he committed treason or something with Timothy Hutton?"

"Yeah, I've never even heard of that film."

"Oh, and he was"—I snapped my fingers—"in that movie they made from that book Cameron Crowe wrote where he pretends to be a high school student, where he actually, I mean Cameron Crowe actually went back to high school and, you know, he wrote that book about the experience and . . . ?"

"Yeah, I don't know what you're talking about," Kip said.

"Oh! And—oh, yeah!—he . . . he was in that movie with Laura Linney where they kill Tim Robbins who's their friend. They think Tim Robbins has done something, I can't remember what, but they kill him, and then they find out it's a mistake. It has the word *mystic* in the title, I think."

Kip was becoming visibly uninterested, which wasn't surprising. A celebrity sighting lives or dies, I suppose, on whether you can actually remember the name of the celebrity.

"It's like Nick Something . . . or Something Nick," I said. "There are like two one-syllable names or . . . he was married to *Madonna*, for chrissakes. Sean Penn!" I said. "It was Sean Penn!"

The name dropped out of my head and onto my tongue like a gum ball dropping out of a gum-ball machine.

"Oh, well," Kip said, straightening up in his chair, "that *is* interesting. I mean, Sean Penn. Now *he's* cute."

"Yeah," I said, although, in truth, none of this made any sense to me. Without Sean Penn's name, the story had no wattage. Without his name, Kip couldn't imagine Sean Penn. He couldn't conjure him up mentally, but now, *with* the name, all Kip was doing was conjuring Sean Penn up mentally, and where, really, was the thrill in that?

This wasn't even the first time I'd seen Sean Penn. I saw him twenty years before in Los Angeles, with Madonna, no less. I mean, *he* was with Madonna. Barbara and I had been walking into Tommy Tang's, a hip new Thai place on Melrose Avenue, when Penn and Madonna, both dressed in white suits, were suddenly standing before us. We passed through the door at the same moment, holding it open for one another, and then they disappeared, whisked off, no doubt, to wherever celebrities are whisked off to, far from the invasive gaze of plebs like me.

"It's like Halley's comet," I say to Kip. "Every twenty years or so, I see Sean Penn. But perhaps even more importantly, every twenty years or so, Sean Penn sees me. You know, he was probably stealing glances at me and wondering, *Hey, there's that guy again! How come I see him every twenty years?*"

"Yeah," Kip says flatly.

I was kidding, of course, but it's possible. I mean, it's possible that Sean Penn has a preternaturally acute photographic recall of faces. Or maybe he's read my books, though I doubt it. They're not the type of books you imagine Sean Penn's having on his nightstand. (I don't really imagine Sean Penn having a nightstand.) Also, I hadn't written any of them in 1985 when we'd last seen each other. In the twenty years since, Sean Penn and I have traveled in quite different circles, it's true. Famous twenty years ago, he's even more famous now. I experience a kind of red-hot envy towards him. Twenty years ago, all I wanted was to live as an artist, supporting myself with my work. Writers, of course, are never as famous as movie stars, but still, I wanted to be as famous as a movie star, and it's always felt a bit of a defeat to have to teach for a living, hiding out in the hinterlands, far from the glamorous coasts.

"I'll take a beer," I told the waitress.

"Pint or a half-pint?" she said, standing over our table.

"Make it a pint," I said.

Kip ordered a pint as well.

I'm not much of a drinker. I might have a little wine with dinner, but not always. Still, when the waitress returned with the beer—a nutty brown ale—it not only tasted great but, since I hadn't eaten much that day, I got a little buzzed, and as Kip and I spoke about syllabi and prerequisites and credit hours, the thought occurred to me, *Ah! So* this *is why people drink in the afternoons!*

I had no idea what I'd been missing. It was amazing to me to think that a person could feel this way every day of his life after four o'clock! When the waitress returned and asked if we'd like another one, I said yes without hesitation; and a half hour after that, when Kip and I parted, and I walked through the little alleyway connecting Everybody's to the parking lot next door, I felt agreeably bibulous, so much so that even the sight of the Denver boot shackled to the tire of my car, along with the garish orange sticker plastered to the driver's window, didn't put a dent in my mood.

"Oh, no!" I cried aloud. "Well, this is not entirely unexpected!" I said to myself. I may even have laughed. The beer had somehow anaesthetized any anger I might have been feeling, coddling it as though it were an infant and keeping it asleep. "But how am I supposed to drive home with such a device on my tire?"

I approached my car.

WARNING! DO NOT ATTEMPT TO MOVE YOUR VEHICLE! the orange sticker shouted up at me, and beneath these and other helpful remonstrations, it supplied me with a telephone number.

I dialed the number on my cell.

From where I was standing next to my car, even in the twilight, I could see into the parking lot of the drugstore across the street. A man was standing over there, and he began waving at me, pointing to his phone, shouting happily, it seemed.

"It's me! It's me!" he cried, waving his arms and pointing to my phone and back to his phone. "You're calling *me*!" he said. "There's no need! I'll be right over!"

I watched as he made his way across the street, snaking through traffic, and soon he was standing before me, a handsome African American man, shorter than I and a bit on the stocky side.

"Ah, so it's *you!*" I said, greeting him like a long-lost friend. "*You're* the one who put this contraption onto my car."

"I did, yes," he said. "It's me!"

"Oh, man," I told him. "I wish you hadn't've done that."

"I know, I know," he said. "Most people, I have to say, feel that way."

"Understandably."

"Sure, sure."

It's hard to explain. We were standing very near each other, smiling into each other's faces. I was feeling lax and limber from the beer. That had something to do with it, I'm sure; but there was also something agreeable about this fellow. He was soft-spoken with a playfulness about him that you don't often encounter in people.

"I'll tell you what. There's a good man," I said. "Unlock the contraption, no hard feelings, and I'll be on my way."

"Well, but I can't do that," he said.

"But of course you can," I said.

"I can't."

"You put it on, didn't you?"

"Yes."

"Well, then I assume you know how to take it off."

"Oh, I do. I do. I know how to take it off. That's my job."

"There you are! You see, you're just the man I was looking for. Because you realize—I'm sure you realize—I can't drive home with that thing on my car."

"No, no," he said, "I wouldn't try it."

"And it's time for me to drive home."

I tapped the face of my watch with my index finger.

"Well, I'd be happy to take it off," he said.

"Happy! See, that makes me happy, too!"

"But you're going to have to pay first."

"Pay first. Right, right. I understand. I mean, I understand *why* you might feel that way. But . . ."

"But what?"

"I'd rather not."

"You'd rather not *pay*?"

"No, yes, I'd rather not pay."

This seemed to amuse him.

"Well, but you parked here illegally," he said.

"No, I was a patron at one of these stores."

"But you weren't. You weren't," he said. "I saw you."

"You were hiding?"

"I was hiding, yes, and I saw you park, and I saw you walk out, and I saw you wander down the street towards those apartments over there."

"That's exactly right," I said. "You see, I had an appointment. I had an appointment with the rabbi at the Chabad House to study Chasidut, although to tell you the truth I'm not really a mystical person. My wife is the mystical person in the family. She can go on and on for hours about the *sephirot* and *chesed* and *gevurah*, and the Garden of Pomegranates, and things like that. We're not really making much progress, the rabbi and I, but I go, I go, and I went today, and yes, when I went today, I parked here and I walked over there, but then I came back and I had a beer, or two beers actually, at Everybody's. And you know who I saw there?"

"Who?"

"Sean Penn."

"Who's Sean Penn?" he said.

"You don't know who Sean Penn is?"

"No, man."

"The movie star?"

"Yeah? Well, I don't know anything about that, but I hope he didn't park here, because, if he parked here, I don't care who he is, he's going to get a boot. This parking lot isn't for Everybody's."

"Yes. Yes, I know that. I know that *now*, you see. I realize that *now*, you see, but I didn't then. So you see it was all an honest mistake."

He smiled an extravagant, indulgent, benevolent and gracious smile.

"What's your name?" I said to him.

"Eugene," he told me.

"Ah, Eugene. It means well born, you know."

"Hey, how did you know that?"

"It's my business to know things like that, Eugene. Now,

Eugene, my parking here was an honest mistake. I had an appointment down the street, as I told you, but I knew I was coming back here, and there *is* a little alleyway—you see it right there—connecting this lot to Everybody's lot, and so it's a reasonable mistake to have made. Now, fun's fun, Eugene, and though I'm enjoying our talk, the hour is late, the day is short. Be a good chap, be a good well-born chap, and take this thing off my car."

"I will," he said. "I'll be happy to do it. I really will. As soon as you pay the fine."

"And what is the fine?"

"Sixty dollars."

"No, Eugene, sixty dollars is excessive."

"But that's the price."

"Yes, that's the price, but it's an excessive price. I'll give you twenty."

Smiling, Eugene looked at the ground, he looked at the sky, at the purpling light of twilight. He seemed as relaxed as I was. He had all the time in the world, I was beginning to realize. He was on the clock, after all, with nothing else to do.

I moved in nearer to him.

"Look, Eugene, I didn't want to have to bring this up, because you seem like a nice person, but your sticker—that garish orange sticker you put on my car—has done considerable damage to my window."

This was true. I'd tried to remove it, and while some of

the sticker came off, some of it didn't, and some of it, in fact, never would.

"I mean, just look at what you've done. I'm afraid there's an eighty-dollar fine. So I'll tell you what: you give me twenty, you take the boot off my car, we'll call it even, and I'll be on my way."

"I'd like to help you," he said, laughing, "but . . ."

"All right, because you seem like a nice fellow, *forget* the twenty. I'll throw in the twenty. There's no need to thank me. Just take the boot off, and we're good."

It was becoming clear to me that Eugene was not going to budge.

"All right, Eugene," I said. "I can see that you're adamant about this. But the thing is"—I shrugged—"I don't have any cash on me."

He pointed with his forehead. "There's an ATM right across the street."

"An ATM across the street?"

"Yeah, across the street, man," he said.

I looked across the street. It was dusk now. The street was a blur of red-and-white car lights.

"At the Noodle House," he added, helpfully.

"There's an ATM across the street at the Noodle House?" I said.

I looked at Eugene. I looked at my car, immobilized by the Denver boot. I looked across the street at the Noodle

House. I thought of my uncle Bernard. I thought of my grandfather. I thought of Sean Penn. Sean Penn wouldn't be arguing with Eugene now. His lawyers or his agents or his managers would be arguing with Eugene on his behalf. But of course, no one would be arguing with Eugene on Sean Penn's behalf, because Sean Penn would never have parked here. His driver would have dropped him off and parked down the road, waiting in a sleekly purring black Escalade for his call.

Some, although not all, of the beer I'd ingested was beginning to wear off, enough, anyway, that Eugene, with his insistence that I pay him, was starting to piss me off. My happy sudsy mood of a half hour before was evaporating. As I crossed the street towards the Noodle House, cutting through the evening traffic, I was aware of two things: first, I was too drunk to be weaving through four lanes of traffic in the near dark, and second, somehow I had made it safely across.

I took sixty dollars out of my account and rewove my way back to the lot.

"There," I said, handing Eugene the cash.

He took some equipment out of the back of his truck, parked nearby. To unlock the boot, he lay down on his stomach on the ground right near my feet. His head was under the car, but I could see his back, his buttocks, and his legs.

"Eugene," I said, standing over him, "I've really enjoyed

our talk today. I really have. You seem like an intelligent, charming fellow. Do you mind if I ask you a question? How is it that an intelligent and charming man like you can't find a better job?"

I seemed to have hit a nerve.

Eugene stood up. No longer so pleasant and good-natured-seeming, he glowered at me, banging the boot and the equipment into the back of his truck. It seemed as though he wished to say something, but instead he climbed into the cab and slammed the door and drove off.

I stood for a moment by my car, feeling terrible. What was *wrong* with me? How could I have said such a thing to another human being?

I drove by the next day, and the day after that, looking for him, hoping to apologize, but I never saw him again: after all, it was his job to hide.

TEN FACES

In the spring of 1995, I published my first short story. We'd gone out to celebrate, and when we returned home the light on our answer machine was blinking.

"S'probably one of my readers calling about the story, don't you think?" I said to Barbara. I was joking, of course. I mention this because many times people don't realize when I'm joking. Many years ago, for instance, my friend Mark McClain and I performed, as a guitar duo, in our junior high school talent show. We had special T-shirts made up for the occasion. Mine said SKIBELL & McCLAIN, his said McCLAIN & SKIBELL. We wanted to give the impression that we were fighting over top billing. It was just a joke, but not long after our performance my eighth-grade English teacher Mrs. Clary cited my shirt as proof that I was, in her opinion, a narcissist.

Why Mrs. Clary thought I was a narcissist and, even more, why she felt it was her duty as my eighth-grade English teacher to tell me she thought I was a narcissist, I no longer recall.

It was probably because *she* was a narcissist and I was insufficiently interested in *her*.

In any case, the T-shirts were just a joke, and it was just a joke when I said to Barbara that the message was probably a reader calling about my story. The story was in *Story* magazine, which was pretty impressive in those days, but I didn't honestly expect anyone to call.

As we listened to the message, though, that seemed to be the case.

Mispronouncing my name, as almost everyone does, shortening the long *i* into a schwa *e*, a woman said she was calling for a Joseph Skəbell and that she wished to speak to him about a matter relating to his family's history and the Holocaust.

Her accent, musical and twangy, was familiar to me from a childhood spent on the West Texas plains. As kids, we use to leave pennies on the railroad tracks, and when we'd come back for them after the train had run through town, they'd look like pocket watches in a Dalí painting. That's what this woman's vowels were like: elongated, misshapen, still recognizable but taking up more space than necessary.

"Curiouser and curiouser," I said to Barbara.

Or perhaps she said it to me.

Because the story I'd published in *Story* magazine was, in fact, a kind of Holocaust-themed fairy tale, chronicling the invented afterlife experiences of my real-life great-grandfather Chaim Skibelski, who had been murdered as a Jew by the Germans during the war.

It seemed impossible to me that I might hear this quickly from a reader, but I was new to the world of small literary magazines, and perhaps I'd underestimated their reach.

I CALLED THE woman back. She sounded relieved to hear from me.

"Oh, thank heavens you've called!" she said. "You have no idea how long I've been waiting to talk to someone from your family! Every time I go *anywheres*, I look through the telephone book for a Skəbell. They's usually none ov'em. But I saw your name, and oh, I just got so excited!"

From the sound of her voice, I imagined her as a simple, countrified woman, over sixty, a bit on the heavy side. In my mind's eye, I saw a cotton print dress, sensible shoes, support hose, wattles beneath her chin, graying hair pulled back into a tight bun, and those cat-eye glasses women used to wear when I was a kid—black rims on the top, translucent rims on the bottom, the design made more feminine, I suppose, by its feline shape. I pictured her standing on a porch out in the countryside somewhere near Palo Duro Canyon, talking on an old black rotary phone, a yellow sunset in a big cloud-filled sky, and no neighbors around for miles.

She introduced herself to me as Mildred Breiner. "But you can call me Millie," she said, and she launched into her story, something about "eleven foster children, who oh my goodness I just loved to pieces." She was so lonesome after her husband, Leonard Sadowsky Sr. died, "an' we never had any chi'dren ov'er own, but they was just all so precious, ever' single one of them. Do you have chi'dren yerself, Mr. Skǝbell?"

As she spoke, I began to realize that the call had nothing to do with my story, nothing to do with my life as a writer, it had nothing to do with me at all. Mildred hadn't read my story. Instead, she told me, "I was searching through the Austin phone book, when I chanced upon your name, and—oh, good Lord Almighty! I been searching for a relative of the artist Skǝbell for, oh, years and years now. Ever since a man named Mac McCluskey walked into my shop in Lockhart.

"Do you have a minute, Mr. Skǝbell? Can I tell you about this?"

It's an occupational hazard, I suppose, or maybe it's just a bad habit I've gotten into, but I tend to listen politely to stranger's stories. I've spoken to a man in a Toronto synagogue who introduced himself to me as the prophet Elijah. I had a long conversation with an elderly woman in a food co-op in Santa Monica about the dangers of miscegenation. ("The blood mixes, you understand, the black and the white blood mix inside the baby, and they fight. The different bloods fight inside the baby and there can be no peace.") I met a woman who told me the electric company was subtly increasing the amount of voltage in her apartment, and when she complained about it, the repairman they sent stole her Bible.

You never know when you might hear something you can use in your work, although to be honest, I've never used any of it so far.

Nevertheless, I told Millie I'd be happy to hear her story.

"Oh, thank heavens!" she said. "You'll never regret it, Mr. Skəbell. I promise you that."

I'm retired now, Millie told me, but for years, I owned a sewing and notions shop in Lockhart, Texas. This was after Mr. Sadowsky, God bless him, passed. And one night, after closing time, it was already dark outside, and I noticed this feller walking back and forth, and back and forth outside my store, peerin' in through the windas, like he couldn't tear himself away. Then he'd tear himself away, but then he'd come back again and start in all over again with his pacin' and his lookin', until I guess he couldn't take it no more and finally he raps on the glass door, askin' to be let in.

Now you have to understand: the door to my back office was open. Which it normally wasn't. Not during store hours leastways. It was my private office, but good Lord! without a word of greeting, this man, a Mr. Mac McCluskey—although at the time I had no idea who he was—well, he just walks in as big as life straight through that store and into that office, right past the sign on the door that says PRIVATE, right up to this black-and-white painting I got hanging on the back wall in there, which he could've seen from the street, but which he couldn't've normally seen since normally that door to my office is shut.

"May I?" he says, and without so much as a word from me, he takes the painting down, and he turns it over and looks at the back of it. "I thought so," he says, and then he says, "Madam, do you have any idea what this painting is?"

Now, good Lord, Joseph, I have no idea what he's talkin' about. It's a powerful painting—that's undeniable—but it's just something I bought at a synagogue art sale in Wichita Falls I don't know how many years ago. I myself am not Jewish, but my husband, Mr. Sadowsky, may he rest in peace, was.

"Ah, my dear lady," this fella says, "allow me to introduce myself to you. I am McCluskey, Mac McCluskey, an art

historian and critic from Austin, and let me tell you something else, my dear, this painting, which you have hung on
the wall of your back office here is . . . a Skəbell."

"A Skəbell?" I say.

"Yes, madam, a Skəbell. That is correct. May I tell you a
little something else about this Skəbell, Mrs. Breiner? Mildred? May I call you Mildred, Mrs. Breiner?"

"Everybody calls me Millie," I told him.

"Millie? Oh, well, all right, then. Fair enough."

ACCORDING TO MILLIE, Mac asked her if she'd
ever heard of the artist Skəbell.

"I didn't think so. Not many people have," Mac said. "He
wasn't well known, despite his enormous talents, even in his
native Europe. Oh, but Millie, this Skəbell, this young man
had a palette and a sense of color that rivaled Chagall's. His
blues were an unheard of blue, his reds a miracle of red!
You've never seen such greens and oranges, to say nothing
of his gelbs and his fuchsias. No one, still to this day, quite
knows how he did it.

"He was a young man when the war broke out," Mac told
her, "and like other young men of the Jewish persuasion,
he joined the resistance. Now, this organization, the underground organization Skəbell joined, was very secretive, as it
had to be. Each cell was made up of only ten men. Only ten
men, Millie, and the nine other men in your cell were the
only other members of the underground you knew, and you

knew these men only by their faces, not by their names. No one knew anyone else's name. The work was that dangerous. Every precaution had to be taken."

And what was the work these men had undertaken?

"They were working with the Swedish diplomat Raoul Wallenberg—you've heard of him, no doubt. No? Well, Wallenberg was helping to smuggle Jews out of Hungary, and the cell Skəbell was in, their mission was to ferry Jewish children out of Europe on boats Wallenberg provided for that express purpose.

"You have to understand, Millie, these ten men had sworn an oath of undying fealty to one another, and their operations, a matter of historical record"—this is true: Wallenberg is known to have saved perhaps as many as a hundred thousand lives—"were extraordinarily successful. That is, until the night their unit was betrayed."

"What happened?" Millie wanted to know.

"What happened, Millie? Exactly. That's exactly the question. What happened? Well, on what proved to be the final night of their work together, Skəbell and his comrades were given ten counterfeit sets of travel documents, *schutzpasses* these were called, enough to carry ten children to safety, but at the last moment, or rather, very nearly at the last moment, Skəbell looked around and saw that they'd collected only nine children. Only nine children, Millie.

"'Where is the tenth child?' he asks his comrades.

"'*You* are the tenth child,' they tell him.

"'Me?'

"'Yes,' they say.

"He protests. Of course, he protests, but they tell him, 'Listen. Now you listen to us. Someone has betrayed us. The Germans know we're here, and soon we'll all be rounded up. There aren't enough identity papers and letters of transit to carry us all to safety.'

"'But we agreed to perish as a group!' he says.

"Now, this was true, Millie. As I said, the members of the cell had bonded themselves to one another with a sacred pledge. With a sacred pledge, they'd joined their fates, their destinies, one for all and all for one, and the idea of abandoning the others in order to save himself alone, even at their request, was hateful to Skəbell.

"'You're the youngest,' they told him. 'Don't you see? You have the best chance of surviving. And more important, you're an artist, you're a storyteller, your paintings tell a story, and you must live to tell our story to the world!'

"The others are in perfect agreement about this, but Skəbell is enraged.

"'How could you have decided this without me?' he roars.

"'Would you have gone if we'd told you in advance?'

"'Certainly not! Just as I won't go now. If we are to die, let us die together, as friends!'

"He's insistent, but the others are insistent as well. '*Some-one must tell our story.*' '*Someone must survive us as a witness.*' '*The world must know, and we've decided that it will be you!*'

"In the distance, Millie, there are sirens. Time is of the essence. If Skəbell doesn't get on that boat and if that boat doesn't sail within the next few minutes, many lives, not merely his own, will be lost. But still he refuses! And so they grab him. They grab him, Millie, two men take him by the arms, two by the legs, and they *fling* him up, they *fling* him up onto the ship, on top of those nine children, where he's restrained by the crew. They have to restrain him. He's so enraged he might otherwise have jumped into the water and drowned.

"Now the ship sails, Millie, and as it does, the distance between the ship and the harbor increases, and Skəbell can see the searchlights, he can hear the sirens of the patrols descending upon his comrades, and—oh!—it's a terrible sight."

"And then what happens?" Millie wants to know.

And then, eventually, according to Mac, Skəbell washes up on the more morally coherent shores of Sweden. He makes his way, after the war, to England and finally to America. Like other Skəbells before him, he arrives in Texas, and he lives in Wichita Falls, a broken man, his health ruined, his mind in tatters, struggling all the while with this sacred mandate he's been given, but which he simply cannot bring himself to perform. He's obligated to fulfill the dying wishes of his comrades, true, but how can he paint, how can he make art, how can he create beauty in a world like ours?

"Oh, it's terrible, terrible, Millie, terrible, yes. Nearly twenty years pass, and for those twenty years, Skəbell never picks up a paintbrush. For nearly twenty years, he never approaches a canvas. But in the last months of his life, Millie, maybe in the last month of his life, Skəbell begins painting again."

Employing a stark palette of blacks and whites—color would have been a concession to sentimentality—he composes a group portrait of himself and his nine comrades, the men with whom he's pledged his destiny, the nine companions of his youth. It's a searing group portrait: ten grim faces staring past the viewer in silent testimony, witnesses to utter devastation. In horizontal lines, a thick impasto suggests a kind of barbed-wire fence cordoning the figures off from the rest of humanity.

"Having fulfilled this single commission," Mac tells Millie, "having kept the promise that had been forced upon him against his will, Skəbell breaks down completely and dies. He dies, Millie."

But before his death—he's an artist, after all—he shows the work to one man, to a single art critic, to someone who will understand what he has made.

"He shows the painting to me, Millie. That's right. He showed the painting to me. He called me up in Austin, and asked me to drive out to Wichita Falls to have a look at this painting of his. When I arrive at this dingy little apartment, he refused to show it to me for more than a few seconds, and he wouldn't let me study it at all. But he told me his story, and he showed me how you could see this story in the ten faces of these men: the death, the concern, the chaos, the terror.

"I never thought I'd see that work again, Millie, and to find it here in your notions shop . . . Oh, Millie," McCluskey tells her, "a painting like this doesn't belong in the back of a shop. It should be in a museum in New York or Jerusalem where everyone in the world can see it!

"Listen, Millie," Mac tells her. "I have a friend in Austin, a gallery owner named Carl Barho, and with your permission, I'd like to mention this painting to him, and together, we'll figure out what should be done with it."

MILLIE, OF COURSE, gave him her permission.

"Who was I to stand in the way of history?" she tells me. "The story touched me so deeply, Joseph, I knew I could never be selfish about it. Skǝbell had been given a sacred mission, and now I was part of that mission, and—oh, Joseph!—with Mac's help, I did ever'thing on earth I could think of on Skǝbell's behalf. I sent a passel of letters and photographs to museums all over the world, and I got a treasure trove of letters back, and I can send them to you, if you want."

She explains: "We wanted to get the painting to somebody who understood what it was and who had the financial wherewithal to ensure that the painting receives the honor it deserves. Mac thought the best person in the world for that was a Dr. Lazlo Tauber. Y'ever hear of him?"

Tauber was a surgeon and a Holocaust survivor from Hungary, it seems. As a young doctor, rather than fleeing Budapest, he remained in the city, tending to the wounded, working day and night in a makeshift hospital, and later, in America, he became a millionaire investor and a noted philanthropist.

"Mac thought Dr. Tauber'd be just the right person to get the painting up somewheres, and I knew in my heart that if we could just show the painting to him, if he could just see it, he'd want to help us, I just knew he would."

Though Tauber was a busy man, a meeting was arranged.

"We were supposed to meet him at O'Hare Airport, in between his flights. That's how busy he was: that was the only time he could give us. So I took the painting up there with my brother—and good Lord, Joseph, was it cold in Chicago!—but we must've gotten our signals crossed, because he never showed up. He never did, and I didn't know what to do then, until I saw your name in the phone book."

WHEN I WAS twenty-three or so, I lived in Taos, New Mexico.

In those days, films were screened almost every night at the Taos Community Auditorium, and on Saturday mornings there was a children's film festival. I remember going one Saturday morning to see *Willy Wonka and the Chocolate Factory*, a film I'd loved as a kid. One of my teachers had read the book to us in elementary school: a chapter each day after lunch. But watching the film now as an adult, I saw it in a different light.

The plot—in case you're unfamiliar with the story— involves five golden tickets hidden in hundreds of thousands of Willy Wonka chocolate bars. These tickets entitle whoever is lucky enough to find one to a trip through Willie Wonka's mysterious candy factory. The first four tickets are found by rich or spoiled or obnoxious children who in no way deserve them, four really terrible kids: Mike Teevee, an early TV addict; Augustus Gloop, a glutton; Veruca Salt, a spoiled rich girl, Violet Beauregarde, a jaw-breaking gum chewer.

Roald Dahl, the author of the book, was said to have hated children. According to legend, he was angry that his success had come to him as a children's writer, that his literary fiction had been rejected by the publishers, and as a consequence, it wasn't hard for him to imagine all sorts of horrible things happening to all sorts of children. He was also supposed to have been a terrible antisemite who was so cruel to his wife, the actress Patricia O'Neal, that she had a nervous breakdown.

I don't know if any of this is true.

There's a fifth ticket, and though its discovery is dramatically delayed, there's never any doubt that Charlie, the film's protagonist and a child whose family is so poor they can afford to buy only one bar of chocolate during the time of the contest, will find it.

And, of course, he does.

I loved the book when I was in second grade, and I loved the film when I was slightly older, but watching it at twenty-three, I realized the sort of thing a twenty-three-year-old watching a favorite childhood movie might realize: that basically we're all Charlies, each of us the protagonist of his own life story, and who doesn't expect great and redemptive things to befall him—a golden ticket!

Now, Millie, it seemed to me, had been given a golden

ticket, and why should her destiny be less remarkable than anyone's? Her story was improbable, but you hear improbable stories like this all the time, stories about a valuable painting left out on the curb as trash and rescued moments before the garbage truck reaches it; stories about rare Beatles recordings turning up in flea markets; the so-called Mexican Suitcase filled with the lost photos of Robert Capa, Gerda Taro and Fred Stein.

What's so remarkable about a historically significant painting being bought at a synagogue art sale and hung on the wall of a notions shop in Lockhart, Texas, where it might be hanging to this very day if an art critic from Austin hadn't been there for God knows what reason?

(I think Millie told me that Mac had been giving a lecture in Lockhart and that he was walking to clear his mind after it or something like that.)

The thought occurred to me that maybe I'd found a golden ticket as well. I'd just started out as a fiction writer. I'd won *Story* magazine's Short Short-Story Contest, it's true, but I'd done so with a tiny little short story, a postmodern fairy tale about the Holocaust. It was barely a thousand words long, and though it was the best thing I'd written, I didn't quite know what to do with it. I mean, I'd have to have written sixty more of these little fairy tales in order to make a book.

But now—now!—thanks to Millie, here was a story with all the themes I'd been working on. Maybe I could write a book about the painting. Or about Skəbell. Maybe I could write a novel about Millie calling me with all these stories about the painting. As a character in the drama, I could investigate the provenance of the painting and research the life of Skəbell. The image of these nine men *flinging* him onto the deck of that ship, that sense of hurtling, of being propelled into flight: *There is something in that*, I thought.

And then another thought occurred to me: *What if Skəbell is Lepke?*

MY GREAT-GRANDFATHER, CHAIM Skibelski, the protagonist of the short short story I thought Millie might have read, but which it seems that she hadn't, had ten children. His four daughters all perished in the war with their husbands and their children. Of the sons, four of them were in America when the war began; and of the two who were left in Europe, only one survived. This was my uncle Sidney. He and his wife, Regina, and his brother Lepke illegally crossed into Russia when the Germans invaded Poland. They were arrested and sent to Russian labor camps and, though Sidney and Regina both survived, Lepke was never seen again.

The only thing I was ever told about Lepke was that he wasn't as *klug*, as smart, as the other brothers who, whether in Poland or America, were all astute deal makers and businessmen. I had originally thought Lepke was mentally slow, but once I was talking to my mother about it, and she suggested that perhaps Lepke simply wasn't as bright in business. All his brothers and his father were bright in business. It was kind of a family trait, and perhaps this is what they meant when they said that Lepke wasn't *klug*.

Now, *I'm* not very bright in business. *I* have no head for numbers. Money is like a foreign language to me. I'm a writer, an artist. *Maybe,* I thought, *that's what Lepke had been. Maybe Lepke was an artist. Maybe Lepke was . . . Skəbell!*

Maybe after all these years, I'd found Lepke!

It made a kind of sense. Separated from his sister-in-law and his brother at the Russian border, Lepke returns home and begins working with the underground, a clandestine cell of resistance fighters, ten men who've pledged themselves to one another, until that fateful night, when, the enemy descending on them, a decision is made: *You're an artist! You're a storyteller! You must live to tell our story!* And they *fling* him on board ship, and like all his brothers before and after him, he makes his way to Texas somehow, where, like his brothers, he shortens his name, Americanizing it from Skibelski to Skəbell. Or rather Skibell (which our family pronounces, against all orthographic convention, as SKY-bell).

What a story! I thought. *What a novel! What this will mean to my family!* All my life they'd told me that I'd never make it as a writer, that no one makes it as a writer, that my dreams were *narishkeit,* foolishness, but now, thanks to me and my *narishkeit,* we'd found Lepke!

THERE WERE ONLY a few problems with this, but they were pretty much insurmountable.

To begin with, Raoul Wallenberg was active in Hungary. Though people were displaced, of course, my family came from Russia, Lithuania, eastern Poland. Secondly: from Millie's description, Skəbell's painting sounded like a painting I'd seen before, and it hadn't been painted by a half-mad resistance fighter either. It had been painted by my cousin Jerry, and it hung in my aunt Norma's living room, a big monochrome canvas with the faces of men staring out from it. Jerry's style, in those days, was sort of Ben Shahn meets Peter Max meets *The Yellow Submarine*, only in muted tones.

I told Millie this.

"Millie," I said, "I think the painting you have was probably done by my cousin Jerry who was born in Texas, like me, and who is still very much alive."

"Well, you never know," she said.

"No, you never do," I said.

"There's always a chance."

"Yes, that's right, Millie, there's always a chance."

"I don't know, Joseph. I still feel like I've stumbled upon something remarkable."

We agreed that she'd send me photos of the painting along with carbon copies of the correspondence she amassed discussing the piece over the years with various Jewish arts organizations and museums.

A FEW OF Jerry's paintings hung in Aunt Norma's living room. They were enormous, or they seemed enormous to me as a kid. One was a huge canvas with five grim world-weary faces staring out of it, a quintet of dour-faced men. They were a little scary, to tell you the truth. And there was a smaller painting of a single face, a similar face, bearded, Israeli-looking, hanging nearby. This smaller picture must have been a lithograph, because copies of it hung in a number of our relatives' homes.

I remember staring at these paintings whenever we'd go to my great-aunt and -uncle's house. We had a lot of family gatherings there when I was a kid. My grandfather was one of Chaim Skibelski's ten children. Three of his sons—my grandfather included—lived in Lubbock, and we'd all get together for Thanksgiving dinners and Passover seders, my grandfather and his brothers, these dark, debonair European men with their accents and their cuff links and their manicures. Their wives and their sons and daughters and their daughters-in-law and their grandchildren would all be at these gatherings. I remember the great social roar of the family, with the women cooking and the men talking business and stocks, my grandfather smoking his big cigars, my father telling jokes, my mother whispering her dry witticisms into my ear, the kids all running in and out of the house.

When you're a child, because you've basically just been dropped into it, you imagine that the world you know is permanent. The adults are like mountains and rivers: part

of the landscape. You can't imagine they were ever different from how you first encountered them, you can't imagine
they were ever young once or trim or unmarried.

And it never occurred to me that our family, which
seemed so large to me, was for my grandfather only half a
family. Though there were five Skibelski brothers in America,
the sixth brother, Lepke, and their four sisters, along with
their husbands and children, never made it out of Europe.

How could Millie be so naive? That's the question, isn't
it? I mean, how likely is it that an historic painting, whose
true worth is unknown, winds up at a synagogue art sale
where it's purchased by a woman who, knowing nothing of
its value, hangs it in her sewing shop in, of all places, Lockhart, Texas, where—ah, but the hand of fate is mysterious!—
it's spotted by the one art historian in the entire world who
knows the true story of its provenance?

Even if it weren't for Jerry's painting, hanging in the gallery of my memory, I'd have been skeptical. It wasn't hard to
be skeptical, and yet, at the same time, I knew from experience that impossible-seeming coincidences happen all the
time.

A few days after my conversation with Millie, in fact,
something equally implausible, if not even more implausible, occurred.

IT WAS THE end of the day, and I was picking
Samantha up at her day care. When I arrived, I noticed that

the children were drawing and painting on the back of a discarded book galley from the University of Texas Press. I turned my daughter's painting over and I saw, on the reverse side, that the text concerned Jackson Pollack, Native American art, and Carl Jung's theory of synchronicity, all of which I knew were the subjects of my friend Jack's dissertation.

As it turned out, one of the day care teachers worked part-time for the University of Texas Press, and the press had recently published Jack's book.

"We didn't have any need of the galley anymore," she told me, "so I brought it in for the kids to draw on. I mean, it's always good to recycle, right?"

"Right," I said.

I thought it would be a nice gesture, and so I sent Jack the picture Sami had drawn on the back of his galley. He called to thank me. He was teaching at the University of Houston at the time, I think, but he grew up in Austin, and he went to the university there, and as we're talking, I said to him, "Hey, let me tell you this weird story."

He's an art historian, after all. He might have some insight into this whole thing. I tell him the story about Millie and Skəbell and Mac McCluskey and Carl Barho, and Jack says: "I know a Carl Barho who was an art dealer in Austin."

"Really?" I say.

"Strictly bluebonnets," Jack says, meaning paintings of fields with Texas bluebonnets in them, meaning Barho sells nothing challenging or serious art-wise. "*And,*" Jack goes on, "I went to high school with a guy named Mac McCluskey, and let me tell you, he was one wild guy, this guy, and his *father*—also named Mac McCluskey—was a maniac. I mean, it's possible he was the kind of guy who would play a dirty trick on a gullible woman somewhere out there in the middle of nowhere."

This was getting weirder and weirder. I mean, talk about your Jungian synchronicities! What were the chances, right? The day-care woman could have chosen any galley to recycle; my daughter didn't have to be drawing when I picked her up, and if she were drawing, she could have been drawing on anything; had she stopped drawing seconds before I arrived, I might never have seen Jack's galley; Barbara could have picked her up that day; the galley sheet she was drawing on could easily not have been recognizable to me as Jack's work; et cetera, et cetera.

ON A WHIM, not too long ago I looked Carl Barho up in the Austin phone book. He still owned a gallery, and was happy to speak with me.

"Oh, yes, I knew the late Mac McCluskey," he told me. "Yes, sir, he and I were good friends." I could hear him drawing on his cigarette over the phone line. "Now, Mac started out as a hamburger cook, but he taught himself all about art, everything there was to know about it, and eventually he owned a gallery."

I brought up Millie and her painting.

"Hm-hm. Hm-hm," he said, listening. "All I can say is that if Mac told this woman the painting she owned was done by a Holocaust survivor named Skəbell, then I'm certain Mac knew what he was talking about, yes, sir, yeah."

I HAD TO wait a couple of days for Millie's package to arrive.

"It's going to take me a little while to get the copies of the photos of the painting made," she told me. I didn't mind waiting. Skəbell had begun to intrigue me. I saw him as a doomed, romantic figure, and even if the story weren't true—*especially* if the story weren't true—I thought maybe I could use it as the basis of a novel, a novel about the loopy effects of distorted history and false memory and our all-too-human desire to fiddle with the past. Maybe I could work in a little something about Holocaust revisionism and maybe even the dangers of Holocaust fiction!

The novel would have two principal characters, Skəbell and me, each of us searching for the other through a foggy corridor of time, he needing me to tell his story, I needing him in order to have a story to tell. The ghost of Lepke would be a part of it. (*Who is Lepke? Where is Lepke? What happened to Lepke? Is Lepke Skəbell?*) Some days I thought this search for Skəbell might change my sense of personal, familial, and even tribal history.

BUT THEN, OF course, the postman drops Millie's package off. It's late spring, and it's hot in Austin, so hot

that perspiration from the postman's hand smudges the ad-
dresses on the letters he's left. I open the package immediately. Along with articles about Raoul Wallenberg and Dr.
Lazlo Tauber, there's a clutch of photocopied letters from
museum curators from all over the world, all dated around
early March 1989:

> Dear Mrs. Breiner . . . thank you for submitting *10 Faces*
> to be considered for possible purchase. The Committee
> has given serious consideration to your offer . . . Thank
> you for your letter. Yes, we agree with your sentiments that
> this piece belongs in a public collection . . . Madam, the
> Museum concentrates almost exclusively on the acquisi-
> tion of art created *in situ* during the period from 1933 to
> 1945. However, may I keep the photograph of *10 Faces*
> for our files?

There are letters from the US Holocaust Museum, the
Jewish Museum in New York, the B'nai B'rith Klutznick Museum, the Skirball Museum, museums in Paris, Jerusalem,
London, letters so carefully worded you can't tell how skeptical the curators are about Millie's claim that the painting
is as valuable as Van Gogh's *Irises*; and certainly, none of
them wanted to pass on it if the painting turns out to be the
real thing.

Along with all of these letters and articles are photos of
the painting, and there they are: those ten faces Millie told
me about, painted in a palette of stark blacks and whites,
each staring grimly out, confronting the viewer, a deeply

beautiful, if unnerving group portrait, reminiscent of Ben Shahn and Peter Max, and clearly the work of my cousin Jerry.

I've kept Jerry updated on the progress of the story, and I forward Millie's package to him along with the photographs. He sends Millie a letter via certified mail, dated April 19, 1995:

> Dear Mrs. Breiner,
>
> First I must verify that I painted the picture in question in 1967 while a student at the University of Texas. How the picture ended up in Wichita Falls, where you purchased it, I can only speculate. The story of the lone Holocaust survivor who wished to memorialize his nine comrades is simply not true. I'm flattered by the value you have placed on my work and it would certainly behoove me to see you obtain such a large sum for the picture. However, now that you are aware that Mr. McCluskey's story is false, I suggest that neither you nor I be party to any such misrepresentation.

I NEVER HEARD from Millie again. All these years later, there are still so many questions. Principally, I wonder: Who was fooling whom? Who was the con man, and what was behind it all? Was McCluskey simply a trickster with a mean streak who sent a gullible woman on a ten-year tizzy? Or was he perhaps mistaken about the painting? Perhaps he'd confused it with another painting he'd been shown. Did he ever really come to Lockhart? Or did Millie simply evoke his name as a way to make her claims about the painting more convincing? Her goals were clear enough: she wanted to sell that painting, either to Lazlo Tauber or to a Jewish museum for a million dollars, or to me. But would she have really invented the whole McCluskey story just to further her aims?

Carl Barho confirmed for me that McCluskey existed, that he was an art critic of sorts and Barho's friend. Still, Millie could easily have found McCluskey's name in the phone book, as she had mine, and invented their conversation. I had to wonder, did she really not read my story in *Story* magazine? Perhaps she'd read my story, noticed that my name was the same name on the painting she owned, and invented a Holocaust fairy tale of her own, this story of Skəbell and the nine others, as a way to jack up the price and sell the painting to me as a precious family heirloom, a bargain at any price. That makes sense, but then she'd have to have forged all those letters from all those curators at all those museums with all their distinctive letterheads almost overnight. Or maybe, having failed years before to entice a museum or Dr. Tauber into buying the painting, she already had everything prepared when she'd read my story.

But that's just too much of a coincidence to believe!

Jerry, as I recall, doubted her sincerity much more than I

did; to me, Millie seemed too simple a woman, too sincere a person to have spun such an elaborate con around a painting she'd apparently owned for years. On the other hand, part of being a con artist, I suppose, is knowing how to appear simple and sincere.

ONCE, FOR EXAMPLE, I was driving home from work—I was a copy editor for a little weekly newspaper in Marina del Rey called the *Argonaut*—and I had to slam on my brakes at a crosswalk in order to let a pedestrian pass. At that time in car-clogged Los Angeles, pedestrians had the absolute right of way, and as I backed up I smiled apologetically at the man, a tall, thin black fellow.

In an instant, he was at my passenger window, knocking on the glass, motioning for me to roll the window down.

"I'm wondering if you can jump-start my car," he said very quickly.

"Jump-start your car?"

"Open the door, go ahead, open the door, and let me in so I can take you to where my car is."

Now, I won't say that I opened that door without thinking, because I *was* thinking, but what I was thinking was that I didn't want this fellow to think I was the sort of person who wouldn't let a stranger into my car simply because he was black. So I was thinking, but I wasn't thinking clearly, and I let him into the car.

"Turn right down there," he said, pointing around the corner. "My car's right down there." Then he said, "Is this a four-volt or a six-volt battery you got here?"

He was asking the wrong person. I had no idea.

"Naw, naw, naw, man, this little Tercel never gonna jump my big ol' American heap. Naw, drive me instead to a gas station, will ya? Service station people'll be able to fix up my car, although," he said, once we arrived at the station, "maybe not in time for me to get to my son in the hospital before visiting hours are through. He's all the way over in Encino."

"Your son's in the hospital?" I said.

"Appendicitis, un-hunh. Come on real suddenlike. He been holt up there for about two weeks now, yes, sir, fighting for his life, poor kid. Say, you don't think you could drive me to the bus station and loan me forty dollars for a ticket?"

I didn't know what to do. I didn't have any money in my wallet. I always forget to carry money, so I drove across Lincoln Boulevard to the nearest ATM machine, and I left the man sitting in my car. He wasn't going to get out of that car. Being in that car was his entire negotiating strategy.

I took twenty dollars out of my account and I stood behind my car, away from the passenger door, but where he could see me. He looked at me. He sized me up. I showed him the twenty-dollar bill. He saw the twenty-dollar bill. He had wanted forty dollars, but this was all I was going to give him.

"Get out of the car," I said, loud enough for him to hear me, "and I'll give you the money."

He looked at the bill again, he looked at me again, he looked at the car again, he looked at me.

I didn't know what he was thinking. I didn't know what he was planning, but I had him at check and there was nothing he could do to get that money except get out of the car. As soon as he stepped out, I threw the bill as far away from the car as I could, and when he went for it, as I knew he would, I ran around to the driver's seat, put my key in the ignition, and drove off.

Now, what strikes me as remarkable about this encounter is the fact that this man was apparently prepared, at a moment's notice, to use whatever circumstances came his way as an occasion for a con. He could never have planned to have been at the crosswalk at the same moment I was. He couldn't have counted on me to treat him as anything more than an abstract blur in my own thirty-five-mile-an-hour landscape. Even less certain were the chances that, acting out of white guilt, I wouldn't have simply driven off or refused to open the door when he approached the car. But somehow in my apologetic nod, in my benevolent we're-all-one-rainbow-nation smile, in the eye contact we made, he saw the perfect alignment of an unanticipated constellation of events, and he was ready, at the drop of that hat, to carry out a con.

Where was he going? Where was he coming from? When

he gets up each day, is it simply his job to walk around from nine to five until he finds someone to bilk?

Or does he just wait for the right set of circumstances to occur?

Did Mac McCluskey do the same thing? Thinking on his feet, seeing that painting on the wall of Millie's shop, perhaps—who knows?—having recently viewed a documentary about Raoul Wallenberg, perhaps he walked into her store with nothing more at stake than the pleasure of fooling a gullible woman. Think about it: he so inflated the value of the painting—if Millie's story is true—there's no chance he could have bought it for himself, which, if he really believed it was that valuable, he could have done for a song, so what other motive could he have had?

On the other hand, maybe Millie read my story, looked at the painting she'd bought at a synagogue art sale years before, and knew there was money to be made here.

YEARS LATER, I'M still wondering. Not too long ago, I called a few McCluskeys in Texas and was told by a Patrick McCluskey that Mac, his uncle, had died at least ten or fifteen years before. "And Aunt Mary, too. It was just too hard for her to live without old Mac, I suppose," he said. "No, sir, un-uhn, I never heard anything about a Holocaust painting."

No one answered at Mildred's old number, although it was still connected. I ran it by an operator at Information who told me it belonged to someone by another name.

There *is* a Mildred Breiner in Houston, but when I spoke to her she said she'd never heard of such a painting.

I left a message at a number for a Carl Barho in Georgetown, Texas, but never heard back.

Most mysteriously, when I asked my friend Jack what he remembered about Mac McCluskey, he claimed to have no memory about any of this at all. When, in an email, I reiterated everything I could remember about Millie and the painting, he wrote me back, saying:

> I *love* these stories of yours, and I promise never to tell your editor that this whole McCluskey thing is (as far as I can tell) a Chagallian hallucination. No, seriously, I think I might remember maybe some parts of this story, but not this MacGuffin or MacLusky part.

The next day, he sent me an additional post:

> Are you sure you've got the name correct? There's an artist who collects art whose name is Milliken. In trying to recall our conversation, his name came into my head. Not so long ago, he gave a collection of African masks to a museum here.

When, under the heading Documentary Evidence, I sent Jack excerpts from a letter I'd written to Jerry in 1995, quoting him as having said that not only had he known Carl Barho, but that he had gone to school with "a Mac McCluskey and a bunch of his siblings" and that it was "possible that this schoolmate might have had a father" who was a bit of a trickster, Jack steadfastly maintained that he never knew Carl Barho personally:

> We used to have some neighbors and his name might in fact have been Carl Barho, but I don't think he was one and the same with the art dealer. I knew a Mac McGarrigle, who appeared to be certifiably insane; I also knew the McCluskey kids, but they weren't weird. I mean, their dad seemed pretty normal, whereas the McGarrigles were really out there.

MacGuffin? Milliken? McGarrigle?

What was going on here?

As I REREAD Jack's email, I found myself wondering where the painting was and whose wall it was hanging on now. I knew it wasn't in a Holocaust museum somewhere, but I wondered if the person who has it, who perhaps inherited it from Millie, knows anything at all about its false history.

Or do even our false histories disappear into smoke?

I asked Jerry once if he remembered the original impulse behind the painting.

"I don't know," he told me. "You draw and you paint and you just start doing things. You start wanting to do a still life, maybe, and it becomes a group of faces. Maybe it emanated from a Beatles album cover, I don't know . . . To be honest with you: you finish a piece and it's there and you might look at it now and then, and it means something different to you now than what it meant back then . . . As for the Holocaust? Well, those faces *are* sort of ominous-looking, aren't they? . . . No, I'll tell you the truth: when I look at that painting today, all I remember is being lifted up by those guys and thrown onto the deck of that ship."

I NEVER WROTE the novel about Lepke. I took the little story about my great-grandfather Chaim Skibelski, the story that had won *Story* magazine's Short Short-Story Contest and which I now think Millie *must* have read, and I made a novel out of it. Not only did my great-grandfather appear in the novel as its protagonist, but my great-grandmother Ester did as well, along with their daughters and their sons-in-law and their grandchildren, all the people who were killed by the Germans.

Even Lepke has a scene or two.

Though these people were my grandfather's parents and his siblings, I never knew much about them when I was growing up. Nobody ever spoke about them or mentioned their names, and I felt that by making them characters in this novel, I was somehow remembering them back into the family, *remembering* them in the normal sense of the word, of course, but also *re-membering* them: making them members of our family again.

MY GRANDFATHER AND his brothers are all gone now; my grandmother and her sisters-in-law, all my great-aunts are gone. It's been years since I sat in Aunt Norma's living room and stared at Jerry's paintings at one of our family get-togethers.

My mother died nearly thirty years ago, and my father more recently. The family has splintered and fractured over the years. That whole big crowd of people moved out of Lubbock and stopped getting together for Thanksgiving. Sometimes we manage a seder, though less and less often now, and when we do, you can almost hear a faint echo of that once-great familial roar.

At my father's funeral, we were all again in Lubbock, the entire family or what remained of it, gathered at his graveside, under those big West Texas skies. We hadn't been together, all of us, like this, in years, but that's how I'd grown up. That was the world I'd grown up in, surrounded by this clutch of relatives, and it feels as though that world's gone forever now.

And that's when it hit me: *Maybe I've finally found Skǝbell*, I thought. *Maybe* I'm *Skǝbell*. Sometimes it feels as though you've just been *flung* into this life, *flung* into life as though it were the deck of a ship that's sailing for a strange and distant land, while the world you know and all the people in it disappear behind you. You arrive with nothing but a story to tell.

If you don't tell that story, it disappears, and even if you do tell it, it might just disappear anyway.